THEATRE

A Theatre5(

IN EVENT OF
MOONE DISASTER

BY ANDREW THOMPSON

In Event of Moone Disaster won the Theatre503 Playwriting Award 2016, and was first performed at Theatre503, London, on 9 October 2017

IN EVENT OF MOONE DISASTER

BY ANDREW THOMPSON

CAST

Sylvia Moone – Past/Present/Future	Rosie Wyatt
Dennis	Thomas Pickles
Neil Moone – Past/Present	Will Norris
Julie Moone	Alicya Eyo
The Doctor/The Lieutenant/William Safire	Dar Dash

CREATIVE TEAM

Director	Lisa Spirling
Designer	Sarah Beaton
Lighting Designer	Ben Jacobs
Composer and Sound Designer	Richard Hammarton
Video Designer	Philippine Laureau
Movement Director	Chi-San Howard
Casting Director	Annelie Powell
Assistant Director	Moses Ssebandeke

PRODUCTION TEAM

Producer	Jake Orr
Assistant Producer	Michelle McKay
Stage Manager	Annette Waldie
Production Manager	Gareth Howells
PR	Mobius. Industries

CAST

ROSIE WYATT – SYLVIA MOONE – PAST/PRESENT/FUTURE
Rosie trained at Royal Welsh College of Music and Drama.

Theatre includes: *Mumburger* (Old Red Lion Theatre); *The Cardinal* (Southwark Playhouse); *Spine* (Soho Theatre; winner Stage Award for Acting Excellence); *The Boy in the Striped Pyjamas* (Chichester Festival Theatre); *Worst Wedding Ever* (Salisbury Playhouse); *Blink* (Soho Theatre/nabokov); *Virgin* (Watford Palace Theatre); *One Man. Two Guvnors* (National Theatre); *Mogadishu* (Lyric Hammersmith); *Bunny* (nabokov) and *Love, Love, Love* (Paines Plough).

Television includes: *Inspector George Gently*, *New Tricks* and *Doctors* (BBC).

Radio includes: *How Did I Get Here?* and *Pride and Prejudice* (BBC).

THOMAS PICKLES – DENNIS
Thomas trained at Rose Bruford College of Theatre and Performance.

Theatre credits include: *The Merry Wives of Windsor/ The Mouse and his Child* (Royal Shakespeare Company); *Blink* (Soho Theatre/nabokov; UK tour and New York); *Treasure Island* (Birmingham Repertory Theatre); *Sign of the Times* (Theatre Royal Bury St. Edmunds); *Dead Party Animals* (King's Head Theatre); *Kes* (Derby Theatre) and *Peter Pan* (Regent's Park Open Air Theatre).

Television credits include: *Casualty*, *Doctors*, *Young Hyacinth* and *Father Brown* (BBC).

Radio credits include: *Blink*, *Stone* and *Real Worlds* (BBC Radio Four).

Thomas is also a writer. His debut play *Dead Party Animals* was named Highly Commended at Soho Theatre's 2013 Verity Bargate Award. The same play then went on to win the inaugural Adrian Pagan Award and received Offie nominations for Best Actor and Most Promising New Playwright. His play *Peacocks* was longlisted for the Royal Exchange's Bruntwood Prize for Playwriting in 2015 and his play *Hymn* was longlisted for BBC Radio Drama North's 2016 Alfred Bradley Award. His first radio drama, *Martha*, aired on BBC Radio Four in May 2017.

WILL NORRIS – NEIL MOONE – PAST/PRESENT
Will trained at RADA.

Theatre includes: *Hamlet*, *The Wind in the Willows* (Creation Theatre); *Macbeth*, *Julius Caesar* (Primary Shakespeare Company); *Barren* (October Sixty Six Productions); *The Rivals* (Mercury Theatre Company); *The Bear, Hard Times, Romeo and Juliet, Under Milk Wood* (REL); *Biloxi Blues* (Couch Potato Productions); *Walk Hard* (Tricycle Theatre); *Who's Harry* (Pleasance Edinburgh & London).

Television includes: *Coronation Street, Heartbeat, Spilt Milk, Rosemary & Thyme, Ultimate Force, The Bill* (ITV); *Dalziel & Pascoe* (BBC) and *Twenty Things To Do Before You're Thirty* (Discovery Channel).

Film includes: *The Theory of Everything* (Working Title); *Swinging with the Finkels* (Serendipity Films); and *Slapper*, directed by Chiwetel Ejiofor.

ALICYA EYO – JULIE MOONE

Theatre includes: *Any Which Way* (Only Connect); *Living Under One Roof* (Theatre Royal, Nottingham); *The Shining* (Royal Court Theatre) and *A Midsummer Night's Dream* (Hopeful Monsters).

Television includes: *Emmerdale, The Bill, Bombshell, Bad Girls* (ITV); *Moving On* (LA Productions); *Justice, Waterloo Road, Silent Witness, Paradox, Casualty, Spooks, Holby City, Doctors, Dear Nobody, Hetty Wainthrop Investigates* (BBC); *Horror House* (MR Productions); *Urban Gothic, A Wing and a Prayer* (Channel 5); *Band of Gold* (Granada).

Film credits include: *The Low Down* (Jamie Thraves); *Greenwich Meantime* (GMT Films); *Tule Tables: Grasshopper* (Horsepower Films); *My Neighbour* (short).

DAR DASH – THE DOCTOR/THE LIEUTENANT/WILLIAM SAFIRE

Dar Dash is an American actor, originally Washington, D.C. He trained at Arts Educational Schools, London.

Theatre includes: *The Glass Cage* (Theatre Royal, Northampton); *Mrs Assad and Me* (Tristan Bates Theatre/Orange Tree Theatre); *The Conference of the Birds* (Folger Theatre, Washington, D.C.); *Scripted* (Tristan Bates Theatre); *Red Light, Green Light* (Old Red Lion Theatre).

Television includes: *Jonathan Creek, The Bill* (BBC); *The Prisoner* (ITV); *Free Agents* (Channel 4).

Film includes: *The Counselor, Warhol* (AOF Best Actor Nominee); *City Slacker, Darkness Into Light* and *Florence Foster Jenkins*.

CREATIVE TEAM

ANDREW THOMPSON – PLAYWRIGHT

Born and raised in Sunderland and following a degree in English, Andrew won a DaDA Award and trained at Webber Douglas. He has spent the following decade working as an actor for companies including the National Theatre and Sheffield Theatres. He started writing and had his first work staged as part of Theatre503's Rapid Write Response nights. Andrew attended the Live Theatre Introduction to Playwriting and an Arvon course before being selected for an Arvon/Jerwood Fellowship, receiving mentorship from David Eldridge. He has had works staged at Arch468, Sheffield Theatres, Chats Palace, White Bear Theatre and The Vaults amongst others. His one act play *Promises* received a run at the Bridewell Theatre in 2015 (Good Picnic Productions) and *The Allotment* received development support from Arts Council England, Poleroid Theatre and Live Theatre, Newcastle. *In Event of Moone Disaster* is his first professional production. Andrew's TV comedy *Spear-Carriers* is currently under option with Hartswood Films.

LISA SPIRLING – DIRECTOR

Lisa Spirling is the Artistic Director and Chief Executive of Theatre503 London. Previously she was the coordinator of the JMK Trust Regional Directors' Programme and a founder of Buckle for Dust Theatre Company.

Directing includes: *Jumpy* by April De Angelis (Theatr Clwyd); *Ken* by Terry Johnson, *Pine* by Jacqui Honess-Martin, *Deposit* by Matt Hartley, *Fault Lines* by Ali Taylor, *I Know How I Feel About Eve* by Colette Kane (Hampstead Theatre); *Hello / Goodbye* by Peter Souter (Singapore Rep); *The Nine O'Clock Slot* (Ice & Fire/Red Gallery); *Donkeys' Years* and *Here* by Michael Frayn (Rose Theatre); *The Garden of Ms Harriet Figg* by Matt Hartley (Old Vic Theatre 24 Hour Plays Celebrity Gala); *Enron* by Lucy Prebble (West End Recast/UK tour); *Idiots of Ants* (Pleasance, Edinburgh/Arts); *Hundreds & Thousands* by Louise Ramsden (Buckle For Dust/English Touring Theatre/Soho Theatre); *Cotton Wool* by Ali Taylor (Buckle for Dust/Theatre503; Meyer Whitworth Award winner); *Terminal Four Play* by Julian Woolford (Theatre503 at Latitude Festival); *Boeing Boeing* by Marc Camoletti (Alley Theatre, Texas); *The Vagina Monologues* by Eve Ensler and *Gas and Air* by Louise Ramsden (Pleasance, London).

SARAH BEATON – DESIGNER

Sarah graduated in 2011 from the Royal Central School of Speech and Drama with First Class Honours. Later that year she was awarded the Linbury Prize for Stage Design. She was the inaugural designer on attachment with the Old Vic between 2015–2016. She is an Associate Artist of Engineer Theatre Collective and a visiting lecturer at the Royal Central School of Speech and Drama.

Design credits include: *Faust* (Schauspielbuhnen in Stuttgart); *Muted* (Bunker); *Don't Panic! It's Challenge Anneka* (Edinburgh Fringe); *Babur in London* (Theatre Rigiblick, Zürich/Lilian Baylis Studio); *Crocodiles* (Royal Exchange Theatre, Manchester); *This Is Living* (Trafalgar Studios); *Mix the Play* (Old Vic & British Council); *Diary of a Madman* (Sherman Cymru/Tobacco Factory); *Nosferatu* (The Lowry, Salford); *And Now: The World!* (Derby Theatre); *Politrix* (Hackney Showroom); *Run, Sold* (Pleasance, Edinburgh); *Missing* (New Diorama, Underbelly); *Yarico* (London Theatre Workshop); *Market Boy*, *The Good Person of Setzuan* and *Macbeth* (Royal Central School of Speech and Drama).

BEN JACOBS – LIGHTING DESIGNER

Ben trained at the Royal Central School of Speech and Drama.

Theatre includes: *Sister* (Ovalhouse); *Maggie & Pierre, Dolphins & Sharks* (Finborough Theatre); *Edward II* (Tristan Bates Theatre); *The State We're In, EleXion* (Theatre503); *People We Didn't Quite Meet, Red, Are We Stronger Than Winston* (The Place); *Cuncrete, Mrs Armitage and the Big Wave* (national tour); *The State of Things, Side by Side by Sondheim, Macbeth* (OFFIE nomination for Best Lighting Design); *Edgar Allen Poe Double Bill* (Jack Studio Theatre); *Free Fall* (Pleasance, London); *Fanny and Faggot, The Lost Happy Endings* (Tabard Theatre).

As Associate: *Project O* (Southbank Centre); *Crave* (Prague Quadrennial), *Miss Sarah* (ZOO Venues, Edinburgh); *Legally Blonde* (Watford Palace Theatre).

RICHARD HAMMARTON – COMPOSER AND SOUND DESIGNER

Theatre includes: *The Weir* (English Touring Theatre); *Assata Taught Me, Comrade Fiasco* (Gate Theatre); *Traitor* (Pilot Theatre); *As You Like It, An Inspector Calls* (Theatre by the Lake); *Faust X2* (Watermill Theatre); *Low Level Panic* (Orange Tree Theatre); *Dirty Great Love Story* (Arts Theatre); *Luv* (Park Theatre); *Orca, Tomcat* (Papatango); *Girls* (HighTide); *Burning Doors* (Belarus Free Theatre); *Much Ado About Nothing, Jumpy* (Theatr Clwyd); *Linda* (Royal Court Theatre); *Crushed Shells and Mud* (Southwark Playhouse); *The Crucible, Brilliant Adventures, Edward II, Dr Faustus* (winner of Men Best Design Award) (Royal Exchange Theatre); *Sunspots, Deposit, Fault Lines, I Know How I Feel About Eve* (Hampstead Downstairs); *Grimm Tales 2* (Bargehouse, Oxo Tower Wharf); *Beached* (Marlowe Theatre/Soho Theatre); *Ghost from a Perfect Place, The Pitchfork Disney* (Arcola Theatre); *The Crucible* (Old Vic); *Dealer's Choice* (Royal & Derngate Theatre); *Kingston 14* (Theatre Royal Stratford East); *A Number* (Nuffield Theatre/Young Vic); *Early Days (of a Better Nation)* (Battersea Arts Centre); *Sizwe Bansi is Dead* (Young Vic/UK tour); *Cheese* (Fanshen); *What Happens in the Winter* (Upswing); *Bandages* (Teg Productions); *The Last Summer* (Gate Theatre, Dublin); *Mudlarks* (HighTide Festival/ Theatre503/Bush Theatre); *The Taming of the Shrew* (Shakespeare's Globe); *Judgement Day* (The Print Room); *Same Same, Little Baby Jesus, Fixer* (Ovalhouse); *Persuasion, The Constant Wife, Les Liaisons Dangereuses, Arsenic and Old Lace, The Real Thing, People at Sea* (Salisbury Playhouse); *Platform* (Old Vic Tunnels); *Ghosts* (Duchess Theatre); *Pride and Prejudice* (Bath Theatre Royal/national tour); *Speaking in Tongues* (Duke of York's Theatre); *The Mountaintop* (Theatre503/Trafalgar 1; winner of Olivier Award for Best New Play); *The Rise and Fall of Little Voice* (Harrogate Theatre); *A Raisin in the Sun* (Lyric Hammersmith/tour); *The Shooky, Dealer's Choice* (Birmingham Rep); *Hello and Goodbye, Some Kind of Bliss* (Trafalgar 2); *Six Characters Looking for an Author* (Young Vic); *Breakfast with Mugabe* (Ustinov, Bath Theatre Royal); *Someone Who'll Watch Over Me* (Theatre Royal, Northampton); *Inches Apart, Natural Selection, Salt Meets Wound, Ship of Fools* (Theatre503); Steve Nallon's *Christmas Carol* (The Door, Birmingham Rep); *Blowing* (national tour/Fanshen).

Film and television includes: *Ripper Street* series 1 and 2, additional music, *No Win No Fee, Sex 'N' Death, Wipeout, The Ship,* five tracks for the accompanying soundtrack album (BBC); *Agatha Christie's Marple: The Secret of Chimneys,* additional music; *Agatha Christie's Marple* series 4, additional music; *Agatha Christie's Marple* series 3, additional music (ITV); *The Pier* (short film; dir.Craig Singer); *First The Worst* (short film; dir. Bevan Walsh); *Raptured* web series (Red On Black Productions); *A Neutral Corner* (Magic Eye

Productions; 2006 winner Kodak Best Short Award); *Konigsspitz, K2, The Fisherman's Wife* (shorts; Discovery Channel); *Snow, The Button* (short films; Magic Eye Productions).

Orchestration work: *Agatha Christie's Marple* series 1 & 2, *Primeval, Jericho, If I Had You* (ITV); *Dracula, A History of Britain, Silent Witness, Dalziel and Pascoe* (BBC); *The Nine Lives of Tomas Katz* (Feature Film, UK); *Alice Through the Looking Glass* (Channel 4); *Scenes of a Sexual Nature* (Feature Film, UK).

Interactive/Digital includes: Foundling Museum (sound installation; The Foundling Museum, London); *Moore Outside* (headphone-based interactive pieces; Tate Britain/Coney); *You Shall Go to the Ball* (online interactive campaign; Royal Opera House); *Light* (interactive installation; BAC).

PHILIPPINE LAUREAU – VIDEO DESIGNER

Philippine Laureau is a projection designer. Philippine graduated from Central Saint Martins School in 2014 and has since worked on a variety of projects in theatre, opera and across the performing arts spectrum. What excites Philippine the most about video design is the myriad of possibilities available to a designer while creating a visual response to the telling of a story. Creative, dedicated and passionate about her job, Philippine is always looking to take on new challenges.

CHI-SAN HOWARD – MOVEMENT DIRECTOR

Chi-San trained at the Royal Central School of Speech and Drama.

Theatre credits include: *Tenderly* (New Wimbledon Theatre Studio); *Cosmic Scallies* (Royal Exchange Theatre/Graeae); *Children of the Night* (Oxford Playhouse/Oxford Arts Festival); *These Trees Are Made of Blood* (Arcola Theatre); *Deposit* (Associate, Hampstead Downstairs); *Occupational Hazards* (Associate, Hampstead Theatre); *Moth* (Hope Mill); *Every You Every Me* (Oxford Playhouse); *The Tempest* (Southwark Playhouse); *Adding Machine: A Musical* (Finborough Theatre); *Narcissus* (RCSSD/Minack); *Scarlet* (Southwark Playhouse); *The Best Pies in London* (Youaremine/RIFT Shakespeare in Shoreditch Festival); *Schumpeter's Gale* (Rose Theatre, Kingston); *Antigone* (Belt Up/UK tour); *Lorca is Dead* (Belt Up/Southwark Playhouse).

Film includes: *Birds of Paradise* (Pemberton Films).

Assistant Movement Director work includes: *Great Expectations* (West Yorkshire Playhouse); *Sweeney Todd: The Demon Barber of Fleet Street* (Welsh National Opera/ West Yorkshire Playhouse).

MOSES SSEBANDEKE – ASSISTANT DIRECTOR

Moses has worked as a writer and director since 2010. He first got involved in theatre through the National Youth Theatre as an actor. He has directed short films that have been shown on national television, and international, in film festivals. He has extensive experience making short films for the BBC, where in 2013 he trained at the BBC Academy. He has worked with BBC Radio Comedy where he shot and edited the promotional video for the 2014 BBC New Comedy Award. As a filmmaker, Moses has worked for BBC Radio One and 1XTRA. Moses was a participant of Theatre503's Five-O-Fresh scheme.

PRODUCTION TEAM

JAKE ORR – PRODUCER
Jake is the Producer at Theatre503.

Producing credits include: *No Miracles Here* (Edinburgh Festival Fringe, The Lowry and Shoreditch Town Hall); *Gutted* (Edinburgh Festival Fringe and HOME); *BLUSH* (Edinburgh Festival Fringe/Soho Theatre/tour); *Weald* (Finborough Theatre); *Shelter Me* (Theatre Delicatessen) and Incoming Festival (New Diorama, 2014–17).

Associate Producing credits include: *Lists for the End of the World* (Edinburgh Festival Fringe); *The Bombing of the Grand Hotel* (Cockpit Theatre/Brighton Fringe); *Mouse Plague* (Edinburgh Festival Fringe/BAC/tour); *The Eradication of Schizophrenia in Western Lapland* (Edinburgh Festival Fringe/BAC/national and international tour).

Jake also founded A Younger Theatre and Incoming Festival and was nominated as Best Producer in the 2014 Off West End Awards.

ANNETTE WALDIE – STAGE MANAGER
Annette graduated from LAMDA in 2007. Recent stage management credits include: *Salomé, Sunset at the Villa Thalia, Behind the Beautiful Forevers* (ASM, National Theatre); *Buried Child* (DSM, ATG); *Jess and Joe Forever* (DSM, Orange Tree Theatre); *Firebird, Pine* (CSM, Hampstead Theatre); *Arrivals and Departures, Time of My Life, The Farcicals, The Importance of Being Earnest, Blythe Spirit* (DSM, Stephen Joseph Theatre/New York); *The Woman in Black* (DSM, Stephen Joseph Theatre; PW Productions); *Life of Riley, A Midsummer Night's Dream, Carmen, Marlene* (ASM, Stephen Joseph Theatre); *F**k the Polar Bears* (CSM, Bush Theatre); *Love Me Do, Fourteen* (DSM, Watford Palace Theatre); *Beauty and the Beast, Snow White* (ASM, Jordan Productions).

GARETH HOWELLS – PRODUCTION MANAGER
Gareth has been working as a production manager for over ten years in London and internationally. He has worked on small- and large-scale tours, site-specific, immersive and new and experimental theatre. On top of his production management work Gareth is the Director of Groundswell Arts, an arts organisation that creates bespoke projects with schools, community and children's centers. This is the first time Gareth has worked with Theatre503 and is enjoying working with a new team.

THEATRE 503

Theatre503 is an award-winning theatre which supports and stages more first-time writers than any other theatre in the country. At the heart of this commitment is a belief that the most important element in a writer's development is to see their work on a stage, in front of an audience, performed to the highest professional standard. Over 100 new pieces of work are staged at 503 in a year, ranging from 1-2 night short pieces to full length 4-week runs. Careers started at 503 include Tom Morton-Smith (*Oppenheimer*), Anna Jordan (*Yen*), Katori Hall (*Mountaintop*), Jon Brittain (*Rotterdam*) – the last two productions started at 503 and won Olivier Awards – and Andrew Thompson himself, who started out with their pioneering Rapid Write Response programme.

Theatre503 Team

Artistic Director	Lisa Spirling
Executive Director	Andrew Shepherd
Producer	Jake Orr
Literary Manager	Steve Harper
Operations Manager	Anna De Freitas
Marketing Coordinator	Rebecca Usher
Technical Manager	Alastair Borland
Literary Associate	Lauretta Barrow
Literary Coordinator	Wayne Brown
Resident Assistant Producers	Helen Milne, Michelle McKay, Pippa Davis
Interns	Holly Dixon, Taylor Dahlberg

Theatre503 Board

Erica Whyman (Chair)
Royce Bell (Vice Chair)
Chris Campbell
Kay Ellen Consolver
Joachim Fleury
Celine Gagnon
Eleanor Lloyd
Marcus Markou
Geraldine Sharpe-Newton
Jack Tilbury
Roy Williams OBE

Theatre503 Volunteers

Aydan Tair, Laura Sedgwick, Shae Rooke, Rob Ellis, Nathalie Czarnecki, Asha Osborne, Emma Griffiths, Carla Kingham, Tom Hartwell, Kelly Agredo, Ceri Lothian, Annabel Pemberton, Uju Enendu, George Linfield, Kay Benson, Angelique Mac-Donald, Ciaran Chillingworth, Amelia Madan, Christina Murdock, Eve Richards, Faaiz Mbelizi, Sussan Sanii, Berit Moback, Dominica Kedzierska, Lucy Robson, Gareth Jones, Emma Anderson, Yasmine Dankwah, Abbiegale Duncanson, Paul Sockett, Sian Thomas, Kai Johnson, Mara Vodinelic, Rachel Tookey, Olivia Munk.

THE THEATRE503 PLAYWRITING AWARD

In Event of Moone Disaster won the second Theatre503 Playwriting Award in 2016. The piece was chosen out of 1629 play submissions from 52 countries. These plays were all read anonymously and rated twice by a team of 20 readers, before 200 plays were longlisted for a further 2 reads. 50 plays were then shortlisted and considered further by the readers and the core Theatre503 team, before a final 5 plays were chosen to be sent to an esteemed judging panel, consisting of Mark Lawson, Timberlake Wertenbaker, Roy Williams, Charlotte Keatley, David Greig, Mel Kenyon, Henry Hitchens and Lily Williams.

Over one long day, Mark Lawson chaired the panel through a passionate discussion of the merits of the 5 final plays before finally voting to reach the decision that has brought this play to your attention.

Theatre503 would like to thank the judging panel and our readers for their dedication, diligence and intuitive engagement with all of the plays we received and without whom we wouldn't be here: Lauretta Barrow, Carla Kingham, Martin Edwards, Tom Latter, Rebecca Latham, Saul Reid, Nika Obydzinski, Joel Ormsby, Anna Mors, Brett Westwell, Carla Grauls, Kate Brower, Tommo Fowler, Sevan Greene, David Benedictus, Nick Cheeseman, Tamsin Irwin, Yasmeen Arden, Tim Bano and Michelle Sewell.

OUR SUPPORTERS

Theatre503's work would not be possible without the support of the following individuals, trusts and organisations:

Our Current Patrons: Angela Hyde-Courtney, Cas & Philip Donald, Darryl Eales, David Baxter, Erica Whyman, Flow Associates, Geraldine Sharpe-Newton, Jill Segal, Kay Ellen Consolver, Marcus Markou, Michael North, Mike Morfey, Pam Alexander and Rotha Bell.

Arts Council England Grants for the Arts, The Boris Karloff Foundation, The Peter Wolff Trust, The Schroder Charity Trust, The Sylvia Waddilove Foundation, Unity Theatre Trust, Wandsworth Borough Council.

Nick Hern Books, The Harold Hyam Wingate Foundation, Curtis Brown and Ben Hall for their support of the Playwriting Award.

The Orseis Trust for their support of the 503Five.

M&G Investments and Barbara Broccoli for their support of our Five-O-Fresh Young Creative Leaders Project. Their support has funded Moses Ssebandeke as Assistant Director on *In Event of Moone Disaster*.

Jack Tilbury, Plann, Dynamics, CharcoalBlue, Stage Solutions, Bush Theatre & Will Bowen for their support in refurbishing our seats.

Theatre503 is in receipt of funding from Arts Council England's Catalyst: Evolve fund, match funding every pound raised in new income until July 2019.

We are particularly grateful to Philip and Christine Carne and the long-term support of the Richard Carne Trust for our Playwriting Award and 503Five.

THANKS

Theatre503 would like to thank Sadie Connelly, Thomas Crowhurst, Laura Morgan, Charles Reston, Trieve Blackwood-Cambridge, Trudi Jackson, Sarah and Elizabeth Mackrory-Scott, Terence Maynard, Geraldine Sharpe-Newton, and 503Friends Members for their support on *In Event of Moone Disaster*.

IN EVENT OF MOONE DISASTER

Andrew Thompson

Acknowledgements

Thanks to:

Lisa Spirling, Andrew Shepherd, Steve Harper and all at
Theatre503 for their dedication in creating this opportunity and
making it all happen, and to the panel of judges for reading my
work and inspiring me with theirs.

Philip, Chris and all at the Richard Carne Trust for their kindness.

The Jerwood Charitable Foundation and Arvon for supporting
new writers with their Mentoring Fellowships and specifically
the guidance and friendship of David Eldridge, Cathy Thomas
and Caroline Gray.

James Grieve for championing me, The Peggy Ramsay
Foundation for scooping a man up when he was down, and
Mel Kenyon for screaming my name from the rooftops.

All those who have read and commented on this script at
various stages.

The cast and crew for climbing on-board with me, my family
for already being there, and especially Viccy and Archer: the
journey to whom inspired so much.

A.T.

For Graeme,
Who shared the start of the story.

Characters

SYLVIA MOONE, *past/present/future – to be played by the
    same young actress*
DENNIS, *past/present – to be played by the same young actor*
NEIL MOONE/THE VOICE
JULIE MOONE
THE DOCTOR/THE LIEUTENANT/WILLIAM SAFIRE
THE ASTRONAUT

Note on the Play

The play takes place between 1969–2056.

Unless specifically stated, all scenes occur in a small northern
English village.

The play consists of a Prologue and Parts One and Two,
containing multiple scenes. New scenes are indicated by (***).

If this break is not used between scenes of differing time
periods then they should be allowed to flow through each other.

Some way of displaying the year to the audience is recommended.

A forward slash (/) at the end of a line indicates overlapping
speech.

A dash (–) at the end of a line indicates interrupted speech.

A lack of punctuation indicates an incomplete expression of
thought.

Text in square brackets [ ] is unspoken.

*This text went to press before the end of rehearsals and so may
differ slightly from the play as performed.*

Prologue

1969

Moonlight

The night of the Moon Landing.

THE ASTRONAUT *stands centre-stage, visor down, looking out towards the audience.*

We hear radio chatter from the Apollo 11 mission.

SYLVIA *enters slowly, watches him, then walks into the arms of* THE ASTRONAUT.

He picks her up gently and spins her round before placing her back on her feet.

They look at each other briefly.

She starts to undo THE ASTRONAUT*'s suit.*

The radio chatter increases. Building in volume and intensity.

They are both now fumbling and pulling at each other's clothes.

A faint, slow countdown starts coming from another room, '10... 9... 8...'

SYLVIA *jumps up and wraps her legs around him, '7... 6...'*

She grinds her body against his. (It is the greatest sex imaginable.) '5... 4... 3... 2...'

'1...' He holds her up into the air.

SYLVIA *floats there. She opens her arms in ecstasy. A moment of beautiful silence. She continues to float upwards, above the head of* THE ASTRONAUT.

Neil Armstrong's speech fills the room:

'One small step for man. One giant leap for mankind.'

THE ASTRONAUT *slowly turns, moves away upstage, and disappears.*

We hear a cheer from within.

SYLVIA *drops suddenly to the floor.*

Blackout.

PART ONE

1969

A Party

Earlier that same evening. DENNIS *is dressed as an astronaut.*

DENNIS. Is it just me or is this bloody amazing.

SYLVIA. You're so pretty, Dennis. Has anyone ever told you that?

DENNIS. There is a *man* on the moon, *our* moon, as we speak and we know cos we can watch it on a television.

SYLVIA. Has anyone ever talked to you about your eyes?

DENNIS. A box. A *box* is showing me pictures of another man actually *in* space.

SYLVIA. I mean *really* talked to you?

DENNIS. Are you alright?

SYLVIA. It's just amazing as you say. What about your lips?

DENNIS. What?

SYLVIA. Your lips.

DENNIS. What about them?

SYLVIA. Exactly.

Beat.

She kisses him.

You taste like… red. Like poppies.

DENNIS. You taste like… have you been sick?

SYLVIA. A bit, yeah. Earlier. It's fine now though, I'm sober. Soberer.

We landed on the moon, you know.

DENNIS. I know. I'm trying to watch it.

SYLVIA. It's *amazing*, isn't it.

DENNIS. That's what I told you.

SYLVIA. What we can do. What we people can do.

We should celebrate.

DENNIS. You have been.

SYLVIA. What do you think it's like, the surface of the moon?

DENNIS. It's a rock, isn't it.

SYLVIA. Wouldn't it be weird if it turned out to be sticky. Or if they'd got there and there was like, one random cow just stood there staring at them. And it just starts grazing.

DENNIS. What would it graze on, / dust.

SYLVIA. Will you do it with me?

It'll be romantic.

She points to the television.

Under the moonlight.

She kisses him again. This time DENNIS *responds.*

They continue to make out sloppily throughout the following.

Oh God.

DENNIS. Yes!

SYLVIA. No, I just thought. What happens if they don't come back. I mean, what would they say?

DENNIS. Who?

SYLVIA. Everyone. That'd be so sad, wouldn't it. Everyone gazing up at the moon and worrying if they'll see a body.

DENNIS. They won't.

SYLVIA *stops.*

SYLVIA. But think of it.

DENNIS *continues, kissing her face and neck.*

All those lovers staring all wide-eyed at the moon. Those moonlit walks and picnics in the park. You and me doing it. They're all of them washed with blood.

DENNIS *stops*.

DENNIS. Is this happening or not?

SYLVIA. I'm just saying, did we think of that, before we sent them.

DENNIS *goes to kiss her again but she stops him*.

Did we realise how much they'd steal from us, those future people all looking badly at the moon. That poor moon. All that time looking longingly at us, dreaming of attention. Touch. Then it happens and they die. The first time you do it with someone and they die on you. I suppose everybody's first time dies, don't they. Eventually. Aw, you've made me all sad now.

DENNIS. I haven't said a word for about five minutes.

SYLVIA (*to the television*). Please don't die, moon people.

DENNIS. Oh God.

SYLVIA. We love you.

DENNIS. Have you taken something?

Beat.

SYLVIA. Bagged it from Bobby /

DENNIS. I knew it /

SYLVIA. It's a funny word /

DENNIS. You always do this /

SYLVIA. 'Bobby' /

DENNIS. Next you'll say you're seeing colours /

SYLVIA. I *am* seeing colours! /

DENNIS. Every time /

SYLVIA. It's like the whole world's in colour /

DENNIS. The whole world *is* in colour /

SYLVIA. My eyeballs are fizzy /

DENNIS. You can't handle it /

SYLVIA. It's amazing.

Dance with me.

DENNIS. Not any more.

SYLVIA. Have a drink with me. Let your hair down. We conquered the universe tonight. Those astronauts, they want us to. They're on that… sticky moon, and they're looking down and they're thinking just… *fuck*. All of you just, everyone just, *fuck*. For us. The whole lot of you. They'll be able to see the earth like, pulsing. I LOVE THIS SONG! Someone turn this up I want the astronauts to hear it. Do you think they will? Do you think they'll hear it? Will we get them dancing?

DENNIS. It would take hours to reach them.

SYLVIA (*indicating TV*). They're right *there*.

Pause.

I'm going to run away. Join a commune.

DENNIS. You won't find one.

SYLVIA. Doesn't matter. Start a commune.

DENNIS. Again.

SYLVIA. This time I mean it.

DENNIS. It'll fall apart /

SYLVIA. We'll experiment with love /

DENNIS. At the same point /

SYLVIA. And states of consciousness /

DENNIS. When you really want a bath.

SYLVIA. A commune in a nice, warm, heated house.

A commune on the moon. I'm going to America.

I'll do it one day soon. I will.

DENNIS. You're on your way down.

SYLVIA. It's wavy.

DENNIS. Why do you take these things?

SYLVIA. It takes me away.

DENNIS. Do you want some water?

SYLVIA. Do you really find me attractive?

DENNIS. You know I do.

SYLVIA. I like hearing that from you. From your mouth.

DENNIS. You never used to.

SYLVIA. People change.

The lighting state flickers.

Will you fuck me please.

DENNIS *doesn't respond. He is frozen. Staring at the television.*

THE ASTRONAUT *emerges.*

SYLVIA *turns and notices* THE ASTRONAUT *as he reaches out his hand.*

She is drawn towards him.

She takes his hand and follows.

***

2017

A Bathroom

JULIE *is sitting on the toilet while* NEIL *sits on the floor.*

NEIL. Let me hold your hand.

JULIE. I need both of them.

NEIL. I'm a part of this.

JULIE. All you've had to do is wank into a plastic cup.

NEIL. Please.

JULIE. I don't want your first memory of our baby to be of me peeing on a stick now get out.

NEIL. But it's momentous.

JULIE. Only the outcome. We don't put the tester in a scrapbook and call it baby's first photo.

Close your eyes at least.

He does.

NEIL. You used to let me watch. Never minded before.

JULIE. This is different.

NEIL. Remember when you were reading your book. And you wanted to finish the chapter but I was desperate. You just opened your legs and let me go in between.

JULIE. Uhuh.

NEIL. Impeccable aim. Would that help?

JULIE. Not right now.

NEIL. We could see if I'm pregnant.

JULIE. You're not helping.

NEIL. I suppose we're lucky it's possible at all. Our parents, our grandparents, would have just had to do without us. We would just never be.

JULIE. Could you talk about anything else.

He opens his eyes.

NEIL. Like what?

JULIE. Eyes!

He shuts them again.

NEIL. My great-grandparents didn't have Granddad until they were nearly our age. That's quite impressive back then.

JULIE. Neil.

NEIL. Sorry.

JULIE. Could you maybe sing or something.

NEIL *sings the first line of 'Space Oddity' by David Bowie.*

– Whistle maybe.

NEIL. You know I can't. You can. Which is interesting. It probably comes from your great uncle who worked on the docks and –

JULIE. Oh God, I don't care about the bloody family tree! Not now. I'm sorry but can I just focus on this for a second.

NEIL. I like learning these things.

JULIE. I know you do.

NEIL. I like putting the family together. It's nice to think we might matter to future generations.

JULIE. I'm trying. To piss.

NEIL. It's about having a family that's mine.

JULIE. And what am I?

NEIL. Flesh and blood. I've none of that. I want them to know who their dad is.

Does fountains help? Or taps? Mum used to say she'd think of Niagra then end up bursting.

JULIE. Your mum's still here you know.

NEIL. Sort of.

She also claimed I came from an astronaut so… It's bollocks obviously but she loved to tell it.

JULIE. It's a good story.

She removes the test, places the lid on it and waits.
Watching it.

NEIL. I used to believe it was true. She said he'd died on the moon. I'd look up and speak to him and know my dad was watching me sleep. Was always there just not always visible. I still prefer sleeping with the curtains open.

JULIE. What happened?

NEIL. You said the street light pissed you off.

JULIE. To the story.

NEIL. I got older. Realised my mum had never left the country. Read books and learnt that no one had ever died up there.

JULIE. What happened when you asked her?

NEIL. She just shrugged and smoked a fag. Now she doesn't remember it. It was never the loss of my dad I missed. It was the loss of the story.

It would be nice to know him. I never used to think that.

JULIE. Find him.

NEIL. Would help me with ours I think. If I met him. Knew him a little.

JULIE. We've got time.

NEIL. Suppose.

Beat.

JULIE. We've got nine months apparently.

He opens his eyes. She holds the test out to him.

Starting now.

***

1969

A Picnic

SYLVIA. Well, look at all this.

DENNIS. I hope you like it.

SYLVIA. What's it for.

DENNIS. For us.

SYLVIA. Us?

DENNIS. I thought about it all. The other night.

SYLVIA. At the party?

DENNIS. Yeah, what we were doing.

SYLVIA. Are those cheese?

DENNIS. You and me.

SYLVIA. I don't like cheese.

DENNIS. There's Spam too.

SYLVIA. That's worse.

DENNIS. I thought about us being something more and I want to.

SYLVIA. I'll just eat the bread.

DENNIS. I'm so glad you think we should.

SYLVIA. Just pick it off.

DENNIS. But I want us to start off on a proper foot. First steps.

SYLVIA. Has this been out a while?

DENNIS. So I thought this was a better date.

SYLVIA. Staler than it looks.

DENNIS. A beginning. The chance to do things properly.

SYLVIA. I'll just suck the butter off instead.

DENNIS. Does that make sense?

SYLVIA. Sorry, what were you saying?

DENNIS. I thought that you and I could spend an evening. As boyfriend and girlfriend. As a test run, nothing too serious and just... see how we feel. Under the moon.

Silence.

SYLVIA. I'm not really hungry.

Pause.

DENNIS. Right.

SYLVIA. Is that a problem? I'll pick at the fruit.

DENNIS. We don't have to eat. It's more the gesture.

SYLVIA. The gesture's nice.

DENNIS. Thanks.

SYLVIA. I like the blanket.

DENNIS. It's from my nana's.

SYLVIA. I recognised it.

DENNIS. I know you like it so

SYLVIA. I do.

Pause.

DENNIS. Should we sit then?

They do.

SYLVIA. So how does this work?

DENNIS. I don't know. We know each other. I guess we just talk.

SYLVIA. About anything?

DENNIS. Anything we want.

SYLVIA. Look at you.

DENNIS. What?

SYLVIA. Being all charming and
      cool.

DENNIS. I'm trying.

SYLVIA. It's very good.

DENNIS. I'm sweating through my vest.

SYLVIA. Come on then.

DENNIS. What?

SYLVIA. Seduce me.

DENNIS. I hadn't realised I was supposed to.

SYLVIA. Tell me…
      what you dream of. For us.

DENNIS. For us? A nice house. Nice car. A family.

SYLVIA. Boys or girls?

DENNIS. One of each. Maybe more.

SYLVIA. What are their names? What'll we call them?

DENNIS. I don't know.

SYLVIA. I like Neil. And Buzz.

DENNIS. What about the girl?

SYLVIA. That's Buzz. Where will we live?

DENNIS. What will our house be?

SYLVIA. Yeah.

DENNIS. A little cottage. Near enough to parents so they can babysit, not so near we see them every day.

SYLVIA. So

here? In the town?

DENNIS. Why not.

SYLVIA. Nothing further out.

DENNIS. I'd have to commute.

SYLVIA. You're not leaving your job?

DENNIS. Why? We'd need to pay the mortgage. All those mouths to feed.

SYLVIA. What about travelling?

DENNIS. Definitely. Family holidays. By the beach. Sticks of rock and kiddies' tears mixed with soft ice cream.

SYLVIA. Is that all?

DENNIS. What more could you wish for?

SYLVIA. Everything.

DENNIS. We'll have everything we could ever want.

SYLVIA. Are you for real?

DENNIS. You sure you won't eat anything?

SYLVIA. I've definitely lost my appetite now.

DENNIS. That's alright.

SYLVIA. Can I tell you something?

DENNIS. Course.

SYLVIA. It's important.

DENNIS. That's good.

SYLVIA. It's gonna hurt.

**

2017

Attic

NEIL. I think I'm getting somewhere.

JULIE. Neil.

NEIL. I thought I'd go through some of Mum's old pictures and it turns out there's a guy keeps popping up and they've got 'Me and D' written on the back of them. I'm guessing he's an old boyfriend, probably American. He looks American. The point is he pretty much disappears once I turn up.

But get this, in some of them he's wearing a NASA jumpsuit. Isn't that incredible. Do you see what this means?

JULIE *doesn't respond.*

The whole astronaut thing may actually have some truth. My dad might actually have been into space.

So.

I reckon they've met, whirlwind romance, but he's been given the call and had to leave, reluctantly, top secret and all that. He never has the chance to say goodbye and unable to return he never learns about me. That's why Mum's stories were always so vague, she had to guess. Wasn't able to communicate with him or learn anything specific but wanted to keep his idea, his ideals alive.

Now. And bear with me here.

While it's too early to tell, I'm building up a profile that could suggest he was Dick Scobee.

Dick was killed in the Challenger disaster, which Mum watched quite a lot about. I remember. I remember thinking it was funny at the time. 'D'. Do you see? I think I've got a real knack for this whole history-detective thing. It's just about educated guesswork to fill in the gaps. It's good, isn't it. Finally a family.

JULIE. I'm bleeding, Neil.

***

1969

A Picnic

SYLVIA. Do you believe in parallel worlds?

DENNIS. I'm struggling with this one.

SYLVIA. I do.

> Till now I used to hate it. The idea there's another me.
> Another version doing better. Living my life better than I am.
> Then I met him.

DENNIS. So why'd you come here. Tonight.

SYLVIA. You invited me.

DENNIS. And you never thought to mention another man.

SYLVIA. I didn't know you were serious.

DENNIS. Yes you did.

SYLVIA. You've put a lot of effort in.

> I thought we were pretending. Like when we were kids.

DENNIS. Did you sleep with him?

SYLVIA. Didn't want to ruin your evening.

DENNIS. Sylvia.

SYLVIA. We barely even talked. It was like

> a silent language.

> He spoke through my bones, my fingers, toenails, eyebrows,
> everything. Everything was just

> fizzing.

> *The lighting state flickers.*

> *She very slowly, but very smoothly, begins to float upwards, a
> few inches off the ground.*

DENNIS. Spoke to your soul.

SYLVIA. Exactly. He's my soulmate.

DENNIS. You've only met him once.

SYLVIA. That's all it takes.

DENNIS. I think those things should grow.

SYLVIA. You're wrong.

DENNIS. Over time.

SYLVIA. Instant. Like mashed potato.

DENNIS. I hate that stuff.

SYLVIA. I love it.

Are you alright?

I'm just telling you what happened.

It's groovy, isn't it. I've met someone. Am I making you jealous?

DENNIS. Jealous! What did you think all this was for?

SYLVIA. It's very nice.

She continues to slowly float upwards.

DENNIS. I wanted to make you feel like that.

SYLVIA. Except the sandwiches.

DENNIS. Look the way your eyes look now, all bright. Then he comes –

SYLVIA. – He did.

DENNIS. He comes and

he can't offer you the world.

SYLVIA. He can.

DENNIS. He *says* he can.

SYLVIA. He did.

DENNIS. I love you.

SYLVIA. I don't care. Not any more.

DENNIS. You can't leave me for him.

SYLVIA. We were never together.

DENNIS. Yes we were.

SYLVIA. Not properly.

DENNIS. You kissed me.

SYLVIA. I fucked him.

Her foot is about his head height. He grabs it.

DENNIS. I thought we had something.

SYLVIA. We did. You do. He just has something better.

She floats there, like a balloon in his hand.

It's like

I'm

DENNIS. Fizzing, I get it.

SYLVIA. But it's more than that.

She's starting to break away. He's trying to keep hold of her.

I can feel it. He can take me away from here, take me to Houston, where it's all happening.

DENNIS. He's not going to Houston, do you hear yourself.

SYLVIA. He is. And he'll take me with him.

DENNIS. Do you even know where Houston is?

SYLVIA. It's not here.

DENNIS. You're off your head.

SYLVIA. I feel alive.

God, why wouldn't somebody want to feel like this!

She releases from his grasp and floats upwards and away in ecstasy.

***

2055

NASA HQ Medical Bay, USA (T (take-off) minus 28 days

THE DOCTOR. Last six presidents?

SYLVIA. Order?

THE DOCTOR. Past to present.

SYLVIA. Obama. Trump. Obama. Johnson. Kushner. Trump.

THE DOCTOR. Still want citizenship?

SYLVIA. It's easier.

THE DOCTOR. Relationship status?

SYLVIA. No change.

THE DOCTOR. No surprise.

   Really, no boyfriend since college?

   What happen, he break your heart?

SYLVIA. I don't want anything that can hold me back.

THE DOCTOR. Last sexual experience?

SYLVIA. I wouldn't exactly call it an experience.

THE DOCTOR. When was it?

SYLVIA. More like wham, bam, thank you, Lieutenant.

THE DOCTOR. Recently?

SYLVIA. Are all the questions going to be so personal?

THE DOCTOR. They are today, yes.

SYLVIA. Did you see my physical scores?

THE DOCTOR. They were very good.

SYLVIA. Outstripped Taylor.

THE DOCTOR. He's been unwell.

SYLVIA. That's cos I got his balls in a jar.

THE DOCTOR. No, actually, I have his balls in a jar.

SYLVIA. Really?

THE DOCTOR. The contents.

SYLVIA. He opted for it then.

THE DOCTOR. They'll be worth a lot of money.

SYLVIA. But for who.

THE DOCTOR. He has a brother to benefit.

SYLVIA. Lucky bro.

THE DOCTOR. Last. Sexual. Experience.

She sighs.

SYLVIA. Wednesday.

THE DOCTOR. Two days?

SYLVIA. A week ago.

He picks up a needle.

And?

THE DOCTOR. I just need some blood.

SYLVIA. What for now?

THE DOCTOR. You know what for.

SYLVIA. You know I'm not.

THE DOCTOR. Procedure.

SYLVIA. I already pee'd on the stick.

THE DOCTOR. Have to be sure.

He begins taking blood.

Still not interested yourself?

SYLVIA. Freezing eggs for a child I'll never meet?

THE DOCTOR. A piece of you left behind.

SYLVIA. Who decides the father?

THE DOCTOR. The highest bidder probably.

He finishes.

SYLVIA. That might be the last prick I ever feel.

THE DOCTOR. You've a little time left to make the most of it before you go.

SYLVIA. My celebrity status.

THE DOCTOR. Most recognised face on the planet.

SYLVIA. Only while I'm on it.

He looks at the results.

THE DOCTOR. There something you want to tell me?

Pause.

SYLVIA. I've never liked that shirt on you.

THE DOCTOR. Sylvia.

SYLVIA. It doesn't suit.

THE DOCTOR. Talk.

SYLVIA. I have an eco-womb.

THE DOCTOR. Who doesn't.

SYLVIA. It's switched off.

THE DOCTOR. Well, something's growing.

Beat.

SYLVIA (*disingenuous*). Can that still happen?

Pause.

So I switched it on, so sue me.

THE DOCTOR. They might.

SYLVIA. I wanted to feel it, okay. Be lunar. For once.

Now I've sold my body to science.

THE DOCTOR. Nobody owns you, Moone.

SYLVIA. The companies do. My whole life I've been a Moone without a cycle.

THE DOCTOR. Most women like avoiding them. With an eco-womb fitted there's no mess, no cramps, no need for protection.

SYLVIA. You sound just like the commercial.

THE DOCTOR. It helps create a level playing field.

SYLVIA. So to be equal I have to turn off my

What my womanhood my, my

gift?

THE DOCTOR. Fine then I'll remove it, shall I.

SYLVIA. God no, you ever had a period, they're horrible.

Pause.

THE DOCTOR. I'm going to reset it now.

And keep this between *us*.

He does.

SYLVIA. What's it matter anyhow, I'm going to Mars. The radiation's gonna make me infertile. And delightfully cancerous. I'm off to conquer a barren world. And be barren while I'm doing it.

Back to his clipboard.

THE DOCTOR. Tell me about your childhood.

SYLVIA. What's to know?

THE DOCTOR. Born in England? Lost your accent.

SYLVIA. Came over here to study.

THE DOCTOR. Don't go back?

SYLVIA. Too difficult.

THE DOCTOR. You've got a licence.

SYLVIA. I'm busy.

THE DOCTOR. It's a shame, what's happened there.

Grandparents.

SYLVIA. What about them.

THE DOCTOR. Maternal.

SYLVIA. Fine. Interfered a lot.

THE DOCTOR. Paternal.

SYLVIA. Never met.

THE DOCTOR. Grandmother had dementia.

SYLVIA. With Lewy bodies.

THE DOCTOR. They named you after her.

SYLVIA. 'Sylvia'. Makes me sound like I'm fucking ancient.

THE DOCTOR. Mom's had a stroke.

SYLVIA. I've been tested.

THE DOCTOR. It's not a problem.

SYLVIA. Then what are you looking for?

THE DOCTOR. Connection.

SYLVIA. To the past?

THE DOCTOR. To keep you here.

SYLVIA. There's none.

Pause.

Was it a boy or girl?

Beat.

THE DOCTOR. Would've been a boy.

Pause.

SYLVIA. At least it's nice to know I could.

Pause.

THE DOCTOR. You speak to your mother?

She shrugs.

Last time in the flesh?

Beat.

SYLVIA. Sixteen months.

THE DOCTOR. For the funeral.

She visit here?

SYLVIA. She can't.

THE DOCTOR. She okay? With all this?

SYLVIA. It's not her decision.

THE DOCTOR. Sylvia.

SYLVIA. Dammit, it's not!

She's seventy-nine. She's well taken care of.

THE DOCTOR. Just checking.

SYLVIA. I told all this to the psych analyst. It's on my file.

THE DOCTOR. I know. Just, as I say

checking.

And you?

SYLVIA. You know I am.

THE DOCTOR. You happy with it?

SYLVIA. Yes!

THE DOCTOR. I have to keep asking.

SYLVIA. I'm happy.

THE DOCTOR. I know. I've seen your press conferences.

SYLVIA. You enjoy them?

THE DOCTOR. You're a natural.

Last excretion?

SYLVIA. Ceased as programmed.

THE DOCTOR. So…?

SYLVIA. Same date as last time.

THE DOCTOR. Which would be…?

SYLVIA. On your form.

He looks at her. She sighs.

Thirteen months.

THE DOCTOR. Eyesight.

SYLVIA. Twenty-twenty.

THE DOCTOR. Weight.

SYLVIA (*groans*). One-forty. And I have ten fingers, ten toes and all of them are wiggling. Toenails, eyebrows, everything.

THE DOCTOR. The attitude isn't helping.

SYLVIA. Sir, yes, sir.

THE DOCTOR. You're mocking me now.

SYLVIA. Sir, no, sir.

THE DOCTOR. Let's keep it casual okay.

SYLVIA. Sir, yes, sir.

THE DOCTOR. Sylvia.

SYLVIA. I'm sorry. It's the meds. The waiting.

He checks her pupils.

THE DOCTOR. You having a reaction?

SYLVIA. No.

THE DOCTOR. Would you say if you were?

Pause.

He carries out basic physical checks – reactions, etc.

SYLVIA. Would you go?

THE DOCTOR. I wouldn't qualify.

SYLVIA. But if you could?

THE DOCTOR. Don't think I have 'The Stuff'.

Beat.

SYLVIA. I'm not going to meet alien beings, you know.

THE DOCTOR. Not intelligent life-forms, no.

SYLVIA. I'm never going to see anyone again.

THE DOCTOR. No.

SYLVIA. Except my crew.

THE DOCTOR. That's right.

SYLVIA. Except on TV screens.

THE DOCTOR. Just the four of you. For ever.

SYLVIA. However long that may be.

***

1969

Outside a Pub

SYLVIA *is drunk and spilling her drink as she gesticulates*.

DENNIS. Congratulations.

SYLVIA. Who said I want to be congratulated?

DENNIS. Most people are happy when they hear it.

SYLVIA. What's there to be happy about?

DENNIS. Life. Starting.

SYLVIA. For who though? Mine's not. Mine's finished, done
    with, over.

DENNIS. You mustn't think like that.

SYLVIA. And where've you been, eh? A whole month and
    I haven't seen you. When I've needed you.

DENNIS. You know why.

SYLVIA. You're my friend.

DENNIS. That boat sailed.

SYLVIA. Was it worth it? Did you get what you wanted?

    So what brings you back here now then?

DENNIS. How far gone are you?

SYLVIA. I don't need you.

DENNIS. You called my house.

SYLVIA. I'm grand.

DENNIS. And the baby?

SYLVIA. What about it?

DENNIS. Is it…?

SYLVIA. Is it fine? I suppose so. Don't matter, I'm not keeping it.

DENNIS. You don't mean that –

SYLVIA. It's going!

DENNIS. Be rational.

SYLVIA. Bit late for all that, isn't it.

DENNIS. Are you sure you should be drinking?

SYLVIA. Why, cos of babies?!

DENNIS. No cos you're getting it all over me.

***

2017

Doctor's Car Park

JULIE. He just asked a lot of questions.

NEIL. And what did you tell him?

JULIE. The truth. I think.

NEIL. You think.

JULIE. I don't remember.

NEIL. You should've let me come in with you.

JULIE. My mind was elsewhere.

NEIL. I'll say.

JULIE. What are you angry at me for?

NEIL. I'm not.

JULIE. I'm doing everything you ask of me.

NEIL. I know.

JULIE. Would it be so bad? We could live our lives.

NEIL. Family matters.

JULIE. I matter.

You could just run off with one of my fertile friends, you know, like a normal person. Malorie. All fat with another one.

NEIL. I don't fancy your friends.

JULIE. Tits to feed an army.

NEIL. Julie.

JULIE. Why not? I would. They're like two bouncy castles stuck sideways on her chest.

That throaty laugh. That throaty, judgemental, 'I'm a lovely mother' laugh.

NEIL. Are you gonna tell me what he said?

JULIE. Bitch.

NEIL. You're in shock.

JULIE. I'm Catholic, you know.

NEIL. Barely.

JULIE. To be infertile's not a sin.

NEIL. I never said it was.

JULIE. I hate her. Hate seeing her. Her brood all

healthy and running around.

Taking over every function, every gathering. All of them. We can never go out and get pissed any more, you know that, don't you. I mean properly bloody trolleyed, without them all judging me. Little darlings have got to be in bed so home by seven.

Judging me for not joining the club. Pitying me for

for everything.

He gets up.

Where you going?

NEIL. To speak to the doctor.

JULIE. You can't just barge in.

NEIL. Watch me.

JULIE. It's just some spotting.

That's what he said. Spotting. It's normal.

NEIL. Well, that's good. That's good, isn't it.

He sits again.

Could've been so much worse.

You get it between periods.

JULIE. Did you ever think you'd be somewhere else by now?

NEIL. But I suppose, when you see blood.

And there's probably others. Many, who ignore it.

JULIE. Probably.

NEIL. And regret it.

You sure you're alright?

Pause.

JULIE. Just take me home.

***

1969

Outside a Pub

SYLVIA. Maybe it'll bring him back to me.

DENNIS. Does he know?

SYLVIA. He'll want proof though. (*To belly.*) We'll keep you till you're big enough to show but then you'll have to hop it, alright?

DENNIS. What if it's not his?

SYLVIA. Why wouldn't it be?

DENNIS. Cos you came to my house, remember.

SYLVIA. Nothing new about that, is there.

DENNIS. Except this time we

SYLVIA. What?

DENNIS.... You know

SYLVIA. I was drunk / so

DENNIS. You weren't drunk /

SYLVIA. I'd been drinking.

DENNIS. Nothing new about that, is there.

   Beat.

SYLVIA. What did we do, Dennis. Or can you not say.

DENNIS. We

SYLVIA. Did we shag.

DENNIS. We're not like that.

SYLVIA. We are.

DENNIS. I'm not.

SYLVIA. Turns out you are.

DENNIS. You shouldn't be so free you know.

SYLVIA. But it's alright for you, is it?

DENNIS. Afterwards, you got up like, like nothing had happened.

SYLVIA. Nothing did happen.

DENNIS. We made love, Sylvie.

SYLVIA. *You* might have, the earth didn't move for me.

DENNIS. You keep acting like we're still only friends.

SYLVIA. It might've even stopped spinning a little –

DENNIS. Fuck you.

SYLVIA. Look at you, swearing all properly. I bring out the best in you.

DENNIS. You could do a lot worse than me you know, you should be grateful.

SYLVIA. I need to do more.

DENNIS. You need to know your place is what you need. Dreams are all well and good but this is reality now and I need you to be honest with me.

Beat.

SYLVIA. I made you a man, didn't I.

DENNIS. Sylvia.

SYLVIA. Yes, my love?

DENNIS. Don't.

SYLVIA. My lover.

DENNIS. Tell me.

SYLVIA. Mi amore?

DENNIS. *Are you having my child?*

She shrugs with a smile.

***

2055

Houston Hotel Room, USA (T-minus 37 days)

SYLVIA *and* THE LIEUTENANT *are facing each other.*
THE LIEUTENANT *should be positioned so we can't really see his face.*

SYLVIA. Don't speak. That's a direct order. I want no speaking, understand?

This is a document. You're going to sign it. You're going to sign it at the bottom and put your initials on the top of each page.

She holds it towards him.

Proceed.

He takes it.

While I respect your sense, I'm not going to stand here and wait for you to read it. Suffice it to say nothing leaves this room and nothing leaves your lips, understand.

You're allowed to nod.

He does.

When this is over, you will know, and you will leave quietly and quickly through the same way you came in.

He nods.

Good.

She begins to undo and remove her shirt.

The agreement states that I require fifteen minutes of your mouth around my clit. I suggest you make your way there via the left breast, that's my left not yours, as it's the most receptive, and though your hands are your own they should be in use at all times – but not for insertion. I'm not fourteen and this is *not* your junior prom. I prefer a sideways motion as opposed to up and down. That's information for your tongue.

After the allotted time I will reciprocate. It will be brief but of sufficient stimulation for you to be active without being cocked to fire. If after the fifteen minutes I am insufficiently wet then God, son, go back to your mother and cry cos I've got no time for amateurs.

You should be stripping. I've no interest in doing that.

He does.

Try to make it appealing but don't try to be sexy. You will fail.

We'll fuck at least twice, I need the exercise. You're allowed to come both times but only early the first time. I'll tell you between sessions if I think I can't. You won't be able to change that but should probably be disappointed with your performance if I don't.

Are those your pants? Your briefs, your underwear?

I don't like them, take them off.

I'll be keeping my bra and pants on for now, it'll be your job to remove them. When doing so delicacy is not my style I'm okay with you just being efficient.

You'll be on top to begin with, I may decide to move things around, you'll go with it. You should remain flexible and responsive, use a degree of your intuition, but I swear to God if you try to take me from behind I will poke you in the eye with my fist. And I don't mean your blue ones. Understood?

Good.

Turn out the light.

THE LIEUTENANT. Would you like to tell me how?

***

The following scenes should flow through each other.

2017

Sylvia's Hospice

SYLVIA *is sitting*.

NEIL. Who's the current Prime Minister?

SYLVIA. Somebody shit.

JULIE. She's right.

NEIL. Can you narrow it down?

   Pause.

   Try it again. A lemon. A toy soldier, and a biscuit.

SYLVIA. Worst. Birthday Presents. Ever.

NEIL. I want you to try and remember them. Memorise.

JULIE. She doesn't remember that she's supposed to remember. Just let her enjoy her birthday.

NEIL. But she remembers it is her birthday, so there's hope. What year were you born?

SYLVIA. Don't be so daft.

NEIL. Tell me and I'll stop asking.

JULIE. The doctors have done all this.

NEIL. Shh.

SYLVIA. I'm not seeing a doctor.

JULIE. Let her enjoy herself.

NEIL. Do you know what year it is?

SYLVIA. Of course I do, don't be so ridiculous.

NEIL. Well?

Pause.

SYLVIA. I've never heard anything so daft.

NEIL. Tell me.

SYLVIA. Fucking ridiculous.

NEIL. Always with the swearing.

JULIE. She can't help it.

NEIL. I don't like it.

SYLVIA. I don't care what you think.

JULIE. Are you hungry, Sylvia? Would you like a tea?

NEIL. She can have something in a minute. Do you remember the name of the lady Prime Minister? In the eighties?

SYLVIA. That bitch next door.

NEIL. She wasn't your neighbour.

SYLVIA. Always judging me. Letting her cat piss in my plant pots. I should bury it. So what if I left him. Got mud all over my slippers.

NEIL. I think we've gone off-topic. Can you name an American president?

SYLVIA. What you wasting my time for? What's he brought me to a quiz for?

NEIL. It's not a quiz. It's to test your memory.

SYLVIA. There's nothing wrong with me.

NEIL. There is.

SYLVIA. My memory is fine.

NEIL. I want you to remember these: A lemon. A toy soldier. And a biscuit.

Beat.

SYLVIA *bites the biscuit.*

He puts it down.

SYLVIA. Disgusting.

JULIE. I'm sure it's not.

SYLVIA. It's mouldy. Gone all soft.

NEIL. It's a Jaffa Cake. You like Jaffa Cakes.

SYLVIA. Doesn't taste the same.

NEIL. It does.

SYLVIA. They've changed them.

NEIL. No they haven't, Mum.

SYLVIA. You saying I'm a liar?

NEIL. No.

SYLVIA. And don't call me that.

NEIL. I didn't say you lied.

SYLVIA. Calling me 'Mum'.

NEIL. You *are* my mum.

SYLVIA. Stop it.

NEIL. You're. My. Mum.

Pause. NEIL *finishes the biscuit.*

Delicious.

SYLVIA. Not the same.

NEIL. Yes, Mum.

SYLVIA. They're not.

NEIL. Course not, Mum –

JULIE. – Neil.

SYLVIA. They've changed the recipe.

NEIL. They have, Mum –

JULIE. – Stop it.

Pause.

SYLVIA *hits him.*

NEIL. Ow… Mum.

And again, harder.

Mum /

JULIE. / Stop it.

And again, harder still.

NEIL. Mum. Mum. Mum.

Each time, she hits him.

JULIE. Neil! You're being cruel.

NEIL. She's hitting me.

JULIE. You're not helping.

NEIL. Neither's hitting.

SYLVIA. It fucking is.

NEIL. Mother!

She hits him. Hard.

JULIE. Stop it! She doesn't know what she's doing.

NEIL. She does. She just doesn't know who to.

JULIE. You're ruining your own visit.

1970

Canteen Kitchen

SYLVIA. What you doing here?

DENNIS. What do you think? I've come to do the right thing. I've come to bloody

to ask you. Will you marry me?

SYLVIA. You what?

DENNIS. Marry me.

SYLVIA. What. Here?

DENNIS. Why not.

SYLVIA. I'm working.

DENNIS. It's romantic.

SYLVIA. It's boiling.

DENNIS. Take a break then.

SYLVIA. I'm cooking carrots.

DENNIS. Do you have to make this so bloody difficult?

SYLVIA. Have you asked my dad?

DENNIS. I will do.

SYLVIA. Coward.

DENNIS. I wanted you to be the first to know.

SYLVIA. Save you wasting a journey.

DENNIS. You matter the most. I mean, you two. The both of you.

SYLVIA. You're not even doing it properly.

DENNIS. Fine, I'll ask him.

SYLVIA. Too late, you've asked me now.

DENNIS. And?

SYLVIA. What? I'm not having it like that. I want you on your knees. I want you on one knee to ask me.

He kneels.

DENNIS. Will you marry me?

SYLVIA. Have you got a ring?

DENNIS. I think so. Somewhere.

He searches himself.

SYLVIA. One thing right at least.

2017

Sylvia's Hospice

NEIL. Where's she off to?

JULIE. Just let her wander. She's stretching her legs.

So, Sylvia, I've done your star chart for your birthday.

NEIL. Why would she care, she's dying.

JULIE. It says here she can anticipate a period of gentle transition.

NEIL. Are you taking the piss?

JULIE. Happiness will also come her way in the form of a new love.

NEIL. Now you're just being ridiculous.

JULIE. No. I took that to mean our '*you know what*'. Thought it would be nice, she'll get to meet it.

SYLVIA. What '*you know what*'?

JULIE. That's your other present, Sylvia. We have some special news.

1970

Canteen Kitchen

He finds the ring.

DENNIS. Right.

SYLVIA. You ready?

DENNIS. Yes.

SYLVIA. Good. Now try again.

DENNIS. Will you?

SYLVIA. I'm not answering that. I want words. Proper ones. With tears.

DENNIS. I haven't…

SYLVIA. How many times do you think this will happen to me?

DENNIS. Right now, none.

SYLVIA. Aw, come on. Make it special. Say

Dear Sylvia Moone…

DENNIS. Dear Sylvia Moone…

SYLVIA. No no, scrap that, I don't like 'Dear', sounds too much like a letter.

DENNIS. What then? Darling?

SYLVIA. Dearest?

DENNIS. My Moone?

SYLVIA. Aw I like that. Mine. Like I'm yours. Makes me feel cared for. You don't own me though.

DENNIS. No.

SYLVIA. Right.

DENNIS. My darling –

SYLVIA. – Just 'My'. I've decided.

DENNIS. My Moone.

SYLVIA *(feigned inquisitive)*. Yes?

DENNIS. I

I don't know what I'm supposed to –

SYLVIA. – You've admired me from afar.

DENNIS. I've admired you from afar.

SYLVIA. And known me up close.

DENNIS. And known you up close – Does that mean –

SYLVIA. – No.

DENNIS. Right.

SYLVIA. And to know you'll be forever in my gaze completes
    me. Or something like that.

DENNIS. And to know you'll be…

SYLVIA. Forever.

DENNIS. Forever in my gaze

    makes me feel so –

SYLVIA. – No!

DENNIS. What?

SYLVIA. Don't improvise.

DENNIS. You said or something *like* that.

SYLVIA. Yeah but I didn't mean it.

DENNIS. Your gaze completes me.

SYLVIA. No!

DENNIS. I can't do this.

SYLVIA. Clearly.

DENNIS. No. This. Like this. Your way, it's weird.

SYLVIA. Well, what do you want then?

DENNIS. You! I bloody want you. And the fact I'm going
    through all this at all must show how much I bloody love you.

SYLVIA. Aw.

He kneels.

2017

Sylvia's Hospice

NEIL. She doesn't understand.

JULIE. She might do.

NEIL. She doesn't know who *we* are, why confuse her further with another one?

JULIE. Because it's nice. We're supposed to be happy.

NEIL. And what happens next time we come?

JULIE. We tell her again.

1970

Canteen Kitchen

DENNIS. You are my Moone. You're a full moon and you're glowing, and I'll care for you. For both of you.

SYLVIA. Bit corny. Which reminds me. Sheila! Drain the sweetcorn!

DENNIS. Stop it! Now listen here –

SYLVIA. – Ooh putting your foot down. Finally a Dennis I can get on board with. Sorry. Go on.

DENNIS. Moone. My Moone. I love you. Will you marry me?

Pause.

SYLVIA (*feigned surprise*). Well, this is all so sudden. I don't know what to say, you've taken me completely by surprise.

DENNIS. Say yes.

Long pause.

2017

Sylvia's Hospice

NEIL. She's gone again.

JULIE. Just keep talking to her. Reassurance.

NEIL. About what, she doesn't know anything.

JULIE. It doesn't matter. It's just nice that we're here.

NEIL. What's the point?

JULIE. Neil.

NEIL. So who are you talking to, Mum?

SYLVIA. He's an idiot.

NEIL. Why, what's he done?

2055

Mars Landing Module

The image appears in close-up via a screen.

SYLVIA. Can anybody hear me!

1970

Canteen Kitchen

DENNIS *and* SYLVIA *start kissing passionately.*

   They begin to tear each other's clothes off.

DENNIS. Are you sure no one's around?

SYLVIA. Just shut up and be inside me.

   They keep kissing.

2017

Sylvia's Hospice

NEIL. Mum?

1970

Canteen Kitchen

They're still kissing.

SYLVIA *lifts her skirt while* DENNIS *fumbles with his trousers.*

2017

Sylvia's Hospice

SYLVIA *is trying to pull her skirt down.*

NEIL. What's she doing! It isn't bathtime now.

    JULIE *feels a twinge.*

    SYLVIA *grunts as if entered.*

    She makes a couple of awkward thrusts.

    Silence.

    …Mum?

    Pause.

SYLVIA. Is that it?

1970

Canteen Kitchen

SYLVIA. I thought this time you might at least…

DENNIS. Sorry.

    Did you?

SYLVIA. Please.

DENNIS. Did you with him?

SYLVIA. An orgasm's like an apology. You never get one from a man.

Silence.

2017

Sylvia's Hospice

NEIL (*gently to* SYLVIA). Are you okay?

1970

Canteen Kitchen

They dress again.

DENNIS. You know you were never more than a fling to him.

SYLVIA. And what are you to me?

DENNIS. I work in a bank. That's good. I'm going to be a bank manager one day, that's respected, that's a real dream.

SYLVIA. I need a man who's going places.

DENNIS. I'm going places. The whole family, we're all of us going to Skegness. You can come too if you want.

You're massive. Do you know that? No one's going to want you now, but I do. I'll have you.

SYLVIA. *Have* me.

DENNIS. I want to do it. You're a free spirit and I love that, but you're bloody stupid and I love that too. One day you'll turn around and I won't be there when you need me.

SYLVIA. I'll never need you.

Pause.

DENNIS. Fine. I'll leave then, shall I.

SYLVIA. You wouldn't.

DENNIS. You want to watch me.

He moves away.

SYLVIA. You'll never leave because you love me, I can click my fingers and you'll be there.

DENNIS. You can't.

She reacts suddenly to a twinge in her stomach.

2017

Sylvia's Hospice

Simultaneously but noiselessly JULIE *reacts to a twinge in her stomach.*

1970

Canteen Kitchen

DENNIS (*concerned*). What? What is it?

She waits till he's close again before standing up, perfectly fine.

SYLVIA. See. And that's why I can never be with you.

DENNIS. You wanted me before.

SYLVIA. It was a mistake.

DENNIS. I don't think so.

SYLVIA. It's pity, Dennis. You're a pity-fuck. Like doing a faithful Labrador, your big sad eyes. I chuck you a frigging bone cos you won't stop panting. That's not

not anything to be proud of. A pity-fuck does not a forever family make.

Silence.

DENNIS. I'll get my coat then.

SYLVIA. Dennis.

If an alien came and said they'd whisk you away a thousand billion miles, to a different planet, but you'd never come back, would you go?

I dream about that.

I dream about lots of things. Mount Rushmore.

I want to rub their noses.

2017

Sylvia's Hospice

NEIL. You're not taking your medication, are you.

SYLVIA. I am.

NEIL. It's here.

SYLVIA. Don't need to.

NEIL. It helps with the visions.

SYLVIA. Make my bones hurt.

JULIE. She doesn't have to if she doesn't want to. They're very powerful.

NEIL. The visions are

disturbing.

SYLVIA. They're not.

NEIL. They are to me.

SYLVIA. They're fucking marvellous. It's like free acid.

JULIE. Not everyone wants what you want, Neil.

NEIL. Mum. Can I ask you about these photos? Mum?

There's photos of you here. With a man. I think he's American. Do you remember?

JULIE. Don't put words in her mouth.

JULIE *twists in her seat.*

NEIL. You okay?

2055

Mars Landing Module

The image appears in close-up via a screen.

SYLVIA. Launch sequence initiated too soon.

2017

Sylvia's Hospice

JULIE. Just uncomfortable.

She continues her discomfort.

NEIL. This American, Mum. You remember him?

JULIE. It is possible your father isn't special, and that's okay.

NEIL. I know but I can feel it. Mum was just that kind of person.

JULIE. Most of them aren't, mine isn't.

NEIL. I know yours isn't.

Mum. Can you tell me who this is? Mum.

JULIE *feels a sudden, sharp pain in her stomach.*

Are you okay?

2055

Mars Landing Module

The image appears in close-up via a screen.

SYLVIA. We're breaking up. I repeat, we're breaking up.

1970

Canteen Kitchen

DENNIS *starts to leave*.

SYLVIA. Dennis, wait.

    He stops.

2017

Sylvia's Hospice

NEIL (*to* SYLVIA). Who's Dennis?

    JULIE *reacts to another pain*.

    (*To* JULIE.) Julie?

    Just breathe.

2055

Mars Landing Module

The image appears in close-up via a screen.

SYLVIA. I'm trying to!

1970

Canteen Kitchen

DENNIS. I'll never ask you again.

2017

Sylvia's Hospice

NEIL. Julie?

    Are you okay?

1970

Canteen Kitchen

DENNIS. Will you marry me?

2055

Mars Landing Module

The image appears in close-up via a screen.

SYLVIA. I don't think we're going to survive this, are we!

2017

Sylvia's Hospice

Silence.

SYLVIA. No.

PART TWO

1985

A Lecture Theatre, Washington State University, USA

WILLIAM SAFIRE. I was asked – by the President no less.
And you don't say no to the President – to prepare a draft.
A statement. I'd proposed it really.

We'd been having meetings about the ergonomics and what
we thought the message of all this should be and I said,
'What if it's not?'

And they looked at me.

And I remember they all looked at me and

it wasn't that it was a unique thought. It wasn't that I'd said
what they hadn't considered. All of them. At one time or
another. It wasn't even taboo, as a topic, it was just

it was the elephant in the room. The thing that no one else
had chosen to notice.

That thought. That same thought had, at one time or another,
entered the mind of every other person in that room – and
I mean all of us – it was just now I'd given it a voice.

'What if it's not?'

'What if they don't? They can't? What if they are *unable* to
come back?'

I mean we had contingencies. We had contingencies for
everything. We had 'em up the yin-yang. Contingencies for
war. Contingencies for nuclear disaster. Acts of God. Hell,
we even knew what we'd do if all the bulbs blew in the
White House at the same time, but this

this was not. In the full sense of the word. 'Prepared for.'

Don't get me wrong. NASA knew what they would do. There were plans. Legitimate, thought out, meticulous plans; and for every step of the way. Every possible thing from a broken chair bracket to complete disaster was considered. It had to be. Remember, it wasn't like today. Like now. We were sending these men up there for the first time with no more technology than exists today in a calculator wristwatch. And that's the truth. Don't get me wrong, that's a mighty fine watch but you wouldn't want it to fly you to the moon and back, though, am I right? It's scary when you think about it now but

that was the reality of the situation. That was where we were in those dangerous and exciting times.

It wasn't that we didn't know what we'd do. It was what we would say. They're gone. Or stranded up there. We've beamed it to the homes of a billion people around the world and now we've got to talk to them. Those people. And appease them. Apologise.

So there I was. At a desk two feet from the Oval Office, only hours away from possibly mankind's greatest achievement, having to write The Speech. Write the words the President would say to the world if all hope had gone.

It wasn't easy, I can tell you.

I poured everything. My heart, my soul, all my fears onto that page. And once it was over

I prayed to God it was never seen or heard of again.

We reached out to touch the Heavens. And I sat down and prayed to God.

*****

2055

Mars Landing Module, USA (T-minus 172 days)

SYLVIA *is strapped into the module, which is shaking dramatically. We can also see her face in close-up via a screen.*

SYLVIA. Can anybody hear me!

THE VOICE (*off*). Can you give us any further information?

SYLVIA. Jesus.

THE VOICE (*off*). Are you okay?

SYLVIA. I'm fine. Just. It's shaking.

THE VOICE (*off*). Can you give us any further information?

SYLVIA. Launch sequence initiated too soon.

THE VOICE (*off*). Concentrate.

SYLVIA. We're breaking up. I repeat, we're breaking up.

THE VOICE (*off*). Just breathe.

SYLVIA. I'm trying to!

Oxygen is flashing. The panel is

I can't think with this damn thing throwing me everywhere.

THE VOICE (*off*). What's your assessment?

SYLVIA. I don't think we're going to survive this, are we!

There is an explosion. The module crashes. Everything becomes still.

SYLVIA *fights her way out of the seat and storms away from it, removing bits of her space suit.*

THE DOCTOR *enters.*

THE DOCTOR. You crashed.

SYLVIA. Not my fault.

THE DOCTOR. It was.

SYLVIA. The programme's glitchy.

THE DOCTOR. No.

SYLVIA. Kept jumping.

THE DOCTOR. Sylvia.

SYLVIA. Fighting me.

THE DOCTOR. You panicked.

SYLVIA. Well, what do you expect!

THE DOCTOR. It's only an exercise.

SYLVIA. It's not my job is what it is.

THE DOCTOR. Everyone on board has to be / able.

SYLVIA. There are others, real pilots who –

THE DOCTOR. We have to be ready for all eventualities.

SYLVIA. It's one chance –

THE DOCTOR. – Exactly –

SYLVIA. – That's all I get. A slip, a a a a a single mistake.
    Human fucking error and it's over.

THE DOCTOR. The people are behind you.

SYLVIA. I don't give a fuck about the people.

    You wanna talk about people that *matter*? His mom, my
    grandma, lived on a shelf for thirty years. Going nowhere.
    Now *he's* mixed in and I...

    All this and he doesn't even know it's happening. And none
    of us might get there and all because of me and

    A fucking urn! That's what they amount to. That's no place
    to fucking sleep.

    Pause.

THE DOCTOR. Maybe you should take a few days.

SYLVIA. Do you think it's genetic? To fail?

    Pause.

THE DOCTOR. I think it's good to practise.

    She starts to re-dress.

SYLVIA. Tell them to reload the programme.

THE DOCTOR. Tomorrow.

SYLVIA. We're doing this now.

                    ***

2017

A Park Bench

Sunset.

The past and present scenes are occurring simultaneously.
NEIL *is sat in the middle.* DENNIS *and* SYLVIA *to his right*
and left.

NEIL. They don't do anything do they. Ducks.

DENNIS. They swim.

NEIL. You can watch a spider spin a web for hours and that's

beautiful.

DENNIS. I hate spiders.

NEIL. Or squirrels. They leap around and look all cute when
chewing nuts, but ducks

they moon you. Stick their arses in the air and wave them at
you. Like kids out the back of a school bus.

DENNIS. They're very maternal.

NEIL. Yes.

DENNIS. Protective.

NEIL. It's nice to see.

Pause.

DENNIS. It's a nice spot, this one.

NEIL. It is.

DENNIS. I'm often here. You meet some interesting people.

Silence.

NEIL. I know who you are.

1973

A Park Bench

SYLVIA *talks to* NEIL. *He is 'present' in the scene but doesn't react.*

SYLVIA. He was an astronaut, you know, your dad. Once he'd finished plundering my natural resources he had to go out looking for more. Someone came along, sabotaged us, took him off the proper course till eventually he got lost. Lost in space.

With a robot for company.

2017

A Park Bench

NEIL. You look just like I thought you would. It's good. It's

strange. I've seen a picture of you. Younger but

…

I thought I'd know what to say right now but I don't.

DENNIS. You and me both.

NEIL. I mean, we must have so much in common.

Little coincidences to unearth.

DENNIS. Your mother is she

He starts to get up.

I think / I'd rather

NEIL. Her mind's not what it was.

DENNIS *sits.*

I mean

who are you?

What did you do?

Pause.

DENNIS. I was a bank manager.

> Branch manager really. Not quite the same any more but all that exists today.

NEIL. That's good.

DENNIS. It was. Once.

NEIL. Needs a strong brain.

> *Pause.*

DENNIS. Do you

> sorry I

> D'you

> work with numbers?

NEIL. No.

DENNIS. Right.

> All automated now. Like working with a robot.

> *Pause.*

NEIL. You've got my nose. Or rather I've got yours.

> *Pause.*

> D'you like sports?

DENNIS. Hmm?

NEIL. Not a big fan of sports. Most people are. We might share that.

DENNIS. I like the rugby. Bit of cricket. Watching the Tests on the telly.

NEIL. I don't really get it.

DENNIS. Right.

> *Pause.*

NEIL. I like dogs.

DENNIS. We've got three cats.

> *Silence.*

NEIL. Books!

I like to read.

DENNIS. Yes.

NEIL. Heavy tomes usually. History. Facts. Biographies of the Greats. Not your lightweight spies-and-fantasy rubbish.

NEIL looks expectantly at DENNIS who smiles awkwardly.

They both look away.

1973

A Park Bench

SYLVIA. Of course he's coming back. One day. For me. He's on a five-year mission, your dad. To seek out new life and new civilisations. Boldly going where no man has gone before.

2017

A Park Bench

NEIL. Just been to Spain. We went after losing the baby.

She likes sangria. My wife. Always ordering it.

DENNIS. I've never really wanted to travel. It's just expected of you, isn't it.

NEIL. Like you're judged if you don't.

Pause.

DENNIS. I'd like to see Mount Rushmore.

Pause.

NEIL. Space.

DENNIS. Hmm?

NEIL. I'd go to space.

You're free up there.

Nobody can own the moon. Did you know that? They made a law apparently. No one country can claim it.

DENNIS. What about a person? Or a business?

NEIL. They didn't put that in. Doubt it matters really.

> You can see everything up there. All your troubles pale into insignificance.

> *Pause.*

DENNIS. I'm sorry about your baby.

> *Pause.*

NEIL. We had a little service at the crem. They say it helps. That and giving them a name, which I don't understand. Seems like then you're surrendering it. When you might have another one. Another go at least. Waste of a perfectly good name.

> Probably shouldn't say that.

DENNIS. It's alright.

NEIL. She looked like a doll. All lifelike. Like a plastic person dipped in ketchup. Everything's there, you know. You don't expect that. Fingers, toenails, eyebrows, everything.

> Glassy, unknowing eyes.

> Actually, could we not

> …

> I'm sorry.

> *Silence.*

1973

A Park Bench

SYLVIA. He *is* the man in the moon. Those craters smiling down, he's in one of those. It absorbed him, made him

> celestial. I'll join him at the end. Be scattered on his skin. So you should never shut your curtains or you'll miss him. It's important. It's important not to miss him.

2017

A Park Bench

NEIL. I had so many ideas about who you'd be. Absurd

fantastical

dreams really. As a kid. Of you swooping in through my window and whisking me off to some space station on the other side of the moon where together we would save the world.

You didn't. Obviously.

DENNIS. I'm scared of heights.

NEIL. But I have to say. Sitting here. None of that matters.

DENNIS. I must be such a disappointment.

NEIL. No. You're blood. I feel it. Pulsing.

I didn't know what I'd feel, but the first thing was how much I wanted to touch you. I know that's strange but

be touched by you. Like a laying on of hands.

DENNIS. I used to hold you as a babe.

NEIL. That must be it! It's like a memory. Burned in to me. Like I can feel it. Would you

I mean. Can I

sorry.

Would it be weird. If I held your hands.

They do.

DENNIS. You need to wrap up warm, you'll catch your death.

NEIL *laughs gently. Transfixed.*

NEIL. I remember this. This skin. I do. I know I shouldn't but I really do.

My dad.

In the flesh.

DENNIS's discomfort increases again.

Do I have

I mean. Have I got

Siblings? A brother? Sister?

DENNIS. This isn't what she wanted.

NEIL. I know we're not '*Father and Son*'. Not properly. It'll take time but

biologically. Chemically.

It's instant, isn't it.

DENNIS. Like mashed potato.

NEIL. I hate that stuff.

DENNIS. Me too.

NEIL. Mother forced it on me.

DENNIS. And me.

They both smile.

You have her eyes. The way you look at me.

NEIL. Cos I've finally found you.

Pause.

DENNIS. I never want to see you again.

***

2017

Rough Guides Head Office, London

JULIE. 'And until next time, "Bon Voyage".'

Beat.

So was that

was that

okay?

Beat. She takes a seat.

[What would you say is the most unconventional thing about you?]

Unconventional? This. I suppose. Looking to travel more. Explore. At my age. Most people are settling down, I've never really wanted that.

[Do you think your age is a factor?]

No cos I could bring more life I think. Traveller's guide through the eyes of a few more miles on the clock.

[Did you practise that?]

Yes I practised that.

[So why now?]

It just feels possible. My family are quite

travelling never spoke to them but me

I think you should push people. Really test yourself.

[And why us?]

It's your ethos I think. You don't take the usual routes. You don't pander to the areas, the companies. You're not afraid to tell the truth.

[Where do you see yourself in five years' time?]

That's the best bit. In five years' time I could be anywhere. From Timbuktu to Tokyo, from Turkey to Taiwan and I

I know you're probably thinking

I don't know, in five years' time I'll be, at home or something. Doing the school run, waving them off at the gates and

Cos I guess that worries you, doesn't it, with my age my, you know, my gender, but you're not allowed to say it any more are you. Out loud I mean.

I'm probably talking myself out of this now aren't I, but it shouldn't matter I suppose, should it.

I mean women, we're told we're free now, aren't we. To do
more I mean. To 'have it all' as they say, without having to
choose, and that's good, isn't it, it's nice, it's just

If that *is* the case

why is it that we can't?

[Thank you.

Could you run through that once more?]

From the top?

She stands.

Straight to the

She points ahead as if to a camera.

'Hi, you're watching Rough Guides. Your friendly Sherpa
through a world of travel possibilities.'

***

2054

NASA HQ Media Centre, USA (T-minus 365 days)

A giant screen is showing the correspondence. SYLVIA *types
and interacts with it by moving her hands.*

> 'What will you do for the journey?'
> @HalsEye

SYLVIA *types.*

> 'Apart from sleep?!'
> @MooneOnMars

> 'LOL'
> @BigAndBold

SYLVIA *types.*

> 'We have experiments with water purity.'
> @MooneOnMars

'The equipment needs to be maintained.'
@MooneOnMars

'We then feed back to MC'
@MooneOnMars

'How does it feel to be chosen'
@AmyHeartsJude

SYLVIA *types*.

'It's an honour. It doesn't feel real. I guess it'll never sink in'
@MooneOnMars

'Until you're standing there.'
@TomsBistro

SYLVIA *types*.

'Hopefully then.'
@MooneOnMars

'What will your purpose'
@SpaceRace

'Sorry'
@SpaceRace

'Sent too soon'
@SpaceRace

'Learn to spell!'
@BigAndBold

'What will your purpose be? On the mission?'
@SpaceRace

SYLVIA *types*.

'I deal in water.'
@MooneOnMars

'I'll be hunting for a source'
@MooneOnMars

'A sign of life. The chance to bring the humans out'
@MooneOnMars

'Keeping us alive.'
@MooneOnMars

'Is it true you came to this through a competition on
a cereal box?'
@TheGuardian

SYLVIA *types*.

'I came to this through my father'
@MooneOnMars

'But the report says…'
@TheGuardian

SYLVIA *waves her arm across and swipes the comment away*.

SYLVIA *types*.

'I know the report.'
@MooneOnMars

'I've worked in this same field my whole life'
@MooneOnMars

THE DOCTOR. You can't ignore their questions.

SYLVIA. They don't matter.

'How do you feel about commercial products paying for
all this?'
@NYTimes

SYLVIA *types*.

'Without them it couldn't happen.'
@MooneOnMars

'Doesn't it bother you our message to the
universe is so corporate?
@GoGreenCorp

'I'll just blow Hershey's Kisses at any Martians I see.'
@MooneOnMars

SYLVIA *pushes her palm forward*.

(*Flashes*.) 'Pause.'

THE DOCTOR. Sponsorship's an issue.

SYLVIA. At least it means their money's going to something. We were going backwards, if a few T-shirts or coffee cups gets us out there than so what.

'Sylvia starts every day with a delicious bowl of Wheaties.'
@WheatiesCerealOfficial

Tata are drilling again. No one's talking about that.

'Buy your special-edition freeze-dried AstorWheats. Just add milk for an out-of-this-world experience!'
@WheatiesCerealOfficial

And we're just letting them.

THE DOCTOR. Companies aren't banned from farming the moon.

'Wheaties. The breakfast of adventurers.'
@WheatiesCerealOfficial

SYLVIA. But only India's benefiting.

THE DOCTOR. You think we won't do the same on Mars.

SYLVIA. We're sharing it.

'Blowing Kisses right back at you Sylvia!'
@Hersheys

THE DOCTOR. We'll see.

SYLVIA. Euro-USA agreement.

THE DOCTOR. Only bits of Europe.

SYLVIA. Most of it.

THE DOCTOR. What about China?

SYLVIA. When they can afford to breathe their own air they can take part in more.

SYLVIA *pushes her palm forward again.*

'Play.'

'Do you like Wheaties?'
@SteveMarshall12

SYLVIA *types*.

> 'I do. The tastiest darned cereal I ever did eat.'
> @MooneOnMars

> 'And yes they paid me to say that.'
> @MooneOnMars

> 'Will you miss your family?'
> @Mumsnet

SYLVIA *types*.

> 'My dad gave up everything to get me here.'
> @MooneOnMars

> 'Introduced me to space.'
> @MooneOnMars

> 'I hope he'll be watching as we fly.'
> @MooneOnMars

> 'Is this for him?'
> @FathersForJustice

SYLVIA *types*.

> 'It's for everyone.'
> @MooneOnMars

> 'Especially those delightful people over at Nesquik.'
> @MooneOnMars

> 'Will you be lonely?'
> @ViccyIsWriting

SYLVIA *types*.

> 'I have a crew. We've bonded.'
> @MooneOnMars

> 'Is there a protocol over disagreements?'
> @SleepyDave

SYLVIA *types*.

> 'Yeah. Don't.'
> @MooneOnMars

'Maybe I'll take some Pedigree Chum. Try make friends with
Mars Rover.'
@MooneOnMars

THE DOCTOR. I think you've made your point.

'Thanks for the mention Sylvia. Mars Milkshakes
available now!'
@NesquikBunny

'Do you know what you'll say when you walk?'
@HillviewPrimary

SYLVIA *types*.

'I'm honoured the TV audience voted me to step out first.'
@MooneOnMars

SYLVIA. Has the line been written yet?

'That cos UR penging!'
@BigAndBold

The last message swipes away and is replaced by.

'This message has been deleted for violation of equality laws
2032 sub-section C.'
@Administrator

THE DOCTOR. Are you wanting to give it away?

'@BigAndBold online status revoked.'
@Administrator

SYLVIA. They've got time to maybe change it.

SYLVIA *types*.

'I probably shouldn't say but…'
@MooneOnMars

'It won't contain commercials of any sort.'
@MooneOnMars

'It'll be a moment purely for mankind.'
@MooneOnMars

That should keep them happy.

THE DOCTOR. Not the sponsors. They're bidding for it.

SYLVIA. I wouldn't say it anyway.

> 'Sylvia. It's your mother…'
> @JulieMoone76

Pause.

SYLVIA *looks at the message.*

SYLVIA *swipes her arm. The message disappears.*

> 'Do you know what they'll say if you don't walk?'
> @UKBackInEuropeCampaign

> 'Yeah. What will they say if you die!'
> @AlexIsFun

Pause.

SYLVIA *types.*

> 'Does it matter?'
> @MooneOnMars

> 'Something nice I hope.'
> @MooneOnMars

***

1970

Hospital

SYLVIA. He wouldn't stop coughing. I was screaming at him but nothing. In the end I brought him here.

DENNIS. You did the right thing.

Pause.

SYLVIA. They had a speech all ready you know. What they'd say if it went wrong. If they lost them. Did you know that?

DENNIS. Who?

SYLVIA. NASA. The Government, the

moon-landers. A whole speech prepared. Just sitting in a drawer ready to announce failure. Loss of life.

I know what I would say.

DENNIS. You won't have to.

SYLVIA. It's too easy to get pregnant.

I think you have to have a plan for the end. Like they must've known what they'd do if they got stuck there. Maybe planned a barbecue.

DENNIS. They'd bunker down and wait for rescue.

SYLVIA. No, they'd die. They'd know that and they would.

DENNIS. You mustn't think like that.

SYLVIA. It's better I think. That way you know.

DENNIS. He's going to be fine.

SYLVIA. I'm not talking about him, I'm talking about me.

I was promised the earth, you know. Literally. They showed it to me. Pictures of it from space and everything.

I hope he's drugged-up.

DENNIS. Any further news, they'll let us know.

SYLVIA. That's how I want to go. Drugged up to the eyeballs.

DENNIS. Why not, that's how you've spent the last five years.

SYLVIA. Imagine, with all our advances, how good drugs will be in the future.

DENNIS. What we could cure with time.

SYLVIA. That too.

Silence.

I don't think I love him. Does that come with time? Cos that's supposed to be instant, isn't it. You push him out and then think 'thank you'. Thanks for tearing me up from arse to elbow, you fat little bastard, I think I love you, now cry. Cry every second of the day cos that's gonna make me love you more, though, isn't it. That's what's normal.

DENNIS. You're tired.

SYLVIA. I am. I really am. Tired of all of it. Tired of waiting for for everything.

DENNIS. What about first steps? Eh? Planting his feet for the first time? That'll be something.

SYLVIA. I keep waiting for him to impress me. He's giggled, blinked, smiled, rolled over, I write them all down.

DENNIS. That's good.

SYLVIA. But I don't care.

I've decided.

She stands up.

DENNIS. What you doing?

SYLVIA. Walking.

DENNIS. You can't just leave him.

SYLVIA. I can.

DENNIS. Sylvia.

SYLVIA. There's plenty of people wanting one. Houses and things to take him. Why do I have to miss out on everything cos of him.

DENNIS. Life's not fair.

SYLVIA. Too right it's not.

DENNIS. Sylvia. Sylvia!

She exits.

***

2017

Adoption Office

NEIL. They won't let us choose?

JULIE. Weren't you listening.

NEIL. But it's my child.

JULIE. She just explained. They use a database. Find the one they feel that we'll suit best.

NEIL. What do they know?

JULIE. They're experts.

NEIL. So you say.

JULIE. They place the one they think will thrive the most.

NEIL. I want to choose the one that's most like me.

JULIE. They don't exist.

NEIL. How do we know? If we can't meet them.

JULIE. We do meet them.

NEIL. We meet the selected ones. The shortlist.

How do we know they aren't just palming us off with someone else's screw-up.

JULIE. They won't.

NEIL. Spawn of Satan.

JULIE. No.

NEIL. I've seen the films.

JULIE. You can't expect to walk into an orphanage and have them all lined up for you to choose.

They're in homes. Foster families. I mean, what would your criteria even be?

NEIL. Smart. Funny. Sporty.

JULIE. It's not a lonely heart.

NEIL. That's exactly what it is.

I want them to be clever. Musical.

JULIE. How could you tell? Will you have them perform for you. Make them dance.

NEIL. Is that possible?

JULIE. No.

NEIL. Well you can tell. By looking at them.

And why can't we have a young one. A baby?

JULIE. Because we can't.

NEIL. But if it's over five it's not really a child.

JULIE. It'll give us a bit more freedom.

NEIL. They're practically giving us an adult and telling us to mother it.

JULIE. It might be younger.

NEIL. It can't possibly be any older, it'll overtake us.

JULIE. It could be siblings.

NEIL. An army of them.

JULIE. Why are you being so negative?

NEIL. I'm being real.

JULIE. You're being *ridiculous*.

Pause.

NEIL. We sell Mum's house.

JULIE. That's paying for her care.

NEIL. She'll live with us.

JULIE. And where does the baby go?

NEIL. We can make it work.

JULIE. I can't, Neil.

NEIL. A surrogate then.

JULIE. No.

NEIL. What's your sister's number?

JULIE. What's gotten into you!

NEIL. I don't want this. That's what.

It isn't us.

JULIE. The combination of us. You and me. It isn't going to happen.

You *have* to accept that.

NEIL. I don't want to feel like a constant babysitter.

JULIE. You won't.

NEIL. Like it's on loan. To be taken back from me.

JULIE. It won't.

NEIL. They're always taken from me.

One more try. As a favour.

JULIE. That's a hell of a fucking favour.

NEIL. I want it.

JULIE. I'm tired, Neil.

NEIL. That's no excuse to quit.

JULIE. I'm old.

NEIL. I love you.

JULIE. Don't bully me!

NEIL. What harm could it do!

JULIE. Apart from pull me apart.

NEIL. It won't.

JULIE. I have a job!

NEIL. I know.

JULIE. No. A new one.

And I want it. More than I ever wanted…

The chance to travel. It's exciting but

it makes having a baby…

Pause.

NEIL. When did you apply?

JULIE. After.

It was after. I swear.

Pause.

NEIL.…Perfect. That's perfect, that'll pay for it then.

JULIE. That isn't what I meant.

NEIL. Why not. The extra money. The life we can provide.

JULIE. Neil.

NEIL. The job's the answer.

JULIE. I would lose it.

NEIL. We can go private.

JULIE. It's a one-off chance.

NEIL. Maternity.

JULIE. I can't do both.

NEIL. They can't take it from you.

JULIE. I won't do both, it would kill the job.

NEIL. Like you killed my child.

Silence.

I didn't mean that.

JULIE. You did.

NEIL. I don't believe that.

JULIE. You said it though.

NEIL. You know I don't.

JULIE. Except you do.

We're finished, Neil. We have to accept that.

NEIL. Not necessarily.

JULIE. It's over.

NEIL. People get lucky.

JULIE. I don't want to.

Silence.

NEIL. I don't want to adopt.

JULIE. We have time to think.

We'll get to travel now. Nice house, nice car. We can have a good life. Touring the world together.

NEIL. What about my mum? I can't leave her. She's all I've got.

JULIE. We'll get her the best.

NEIL. So she can still move in with us?

JULIE. If you want her to.

NEIL. And your parents?

JULIE. They'll understand. It'll take some getting used to.

Pause.

NEIL. And you can be happy?

JULIE. I can now, yes. This is what I want.

Pause.

I'm sorry about your father.

Silence.

NEIL. So, travelling?

JULIE. Yes.

NEIL. Can we see Mount Rushmore? I don't know why.

JULIE. It's done. First thing on the list.

Pause.

So we're really doing this. We're stopping. Now.

NEIL....

JULIE. I need you to be sure.

Beat.

NEIL. It's good that you're happy.

***

1970

Sylvia's Home

DENNIS. He's down now. Do you want to see him?

Pause.

SYLVIA. I'll let him sleep.

DENNIS. Fed him his formula so took a bit of burping.

Shouldn't disrupt him too much.

You should eat too.

I could cook you something.

She shakes her head.

Nobody knows you know.

The neighbours thought it strange it was me brought him home from hospital but I said you were too distraught to face it.

SYLVIA. You're a good dad to him. You're kind.

DENNIS. I'm keeping him alive.

Have your folks been round?

SYLVIA. They're not talking to me.

DENNIS. I'll speak to them.

Do you want me to stay? I can if you like.

SYLVIA. You've got work in the morning.

DENNIS. That's alright.

Pause.

I'll come round after, then. Check on him.

Pause.

There's some mince in the fridge.

Potatoes.

I could peel them for you.

Pause.

I'll be leaving then?

Silence.

He's got your eyes, you know. Every time I look at him I see you staring back at me all bright and

it's amazing really. What you've done.

What we're doing.

It may not be normal but / together we're

SYLVIA. He's not yours, Dennis.

Pause.

DENNIS. He only came a little early.

SYLVIA. Not as early as you did. Twice.

DENNIS. Still manage to cut, don't you.

SYLVIA. You were finished before we'd even gotten started.

DENNIS. I'm still here now though. That's more than some people.

SYLVIA. I was already late before we

you and me, before we ever

Why else do you think I was drinking?

DENNIS. We could lie.

She shakes her head.

The world doesn't need to know. I'll do it anyway.

SYLVIA. It's not fair.

DENNIS. On me? I don't care.

SYLVIA. On him.

Pause.

DENNIS. I saw him you know. Your party boy. Your 'astronaut'. Down the pub with his arm round some dolly bird.

SYLVIA. He'll come again for me.

DENNIS. Does he even know?

Pause.

So what will you tell him? When he's older?

She shrugs again.

He deserves something.

SYLVIA. Not your job.

DENNIS. You're all I can ever think of. That thing, that boy in there, mine / or not

SYLVIA. He's not /

DENNIS. I would do for him. Raise him up proper. As my own. To be with you.

But you don't want that.

SYLVIA. I don't.

DENNIS. Your eyes in his head. They pierce me.

Pause.

SYLVIA. Do you love me, Dennis?

DENNIS. You know I do.

SYLVIA. Then leave.

If you love me, go as far away as possible. And don't come back. For either of us.

That's all I ever want from you.

Silence.

He fades away.

No one should have to stay.

***

2018

Mount Rushmore, USA

They're standing, looking out.

JULIE. And?

NEIL. It's nice.

JULIE. It is.

Silence.

NEIL. It's not as good as I thought it would be.

JULIE. And we're in the middle of bloody nowhere.

Pause.

They smile and hold hands.

NEIL. That little kid looks happy. Over there.

She releases his hand. Looking out.

She places her hand on her stomach.

***

2054

Church (T-minus 527 days)

SYLVIA. You look nice.

JULIE. Thank you.

SYLVIA. It was a lovely service.

JULIE. Too religious for me.

SYLVIA. I liked it.

JULIE. Your father wouldn't.

SYLVIA. I wouldn't know.

Pause.

JULIE. The wiring's gone. My elbow. Makes it heavy. Like having the stroke again.

SYLVIA. And your mind?

JULIE. It's wavy.

Should get them looked at.

SYLVIA. You should.

JULIE. Easier said than done. I've time now I suppose.

Pause.

SYLVIA. Sparser than I expected.

JULIE. He was never flush with friends.

SYLVIA. I meant the church in general, the town. It's shabby.

JULIE *shrugs*.

JULIE. No issues at the borders then?

They say it's even tighter now. We don't even try any more –

SYLVIA. Why didn't you tell me he was sick?

Beat.

JULIE. I guess

we didn't know, we didn't think –

SYLVIA. – Bullshit.

JULIE. You spoke to him. On your screen.

We liked seeing you on the news, you know. You were in Africa.

SYLVIA. I could have been here. In the flesh. Holding his hand.

JULIE. I held it for you.

SYLVIA. He was dying, Mom.

JULIE. He understood.

SYLVIA. He was my father.

JULIE. And you want me to be sorry.

Is that it?

You want me to feel guilty because you saw the sunrise over God knows where while I had to sit here and watch him

I saved you, you know that, don't you.

SYLVIA. Saved me?

JULIE. Saved you from a life of –

SYLVIA. – You sent me away.

JULIE. You asked us to. It's what you wanted or have you conveniently forgotten that. You had so much promise so we scrimped and saved to make it happen for you.

SYLVIA. I was barely a child.

JULIE. And look what you've become. Look at this place. What's happened to it. The buildings, the people the

everything. The smart ones, they ran. Every plane and boat out of here, they were running and I

we

It wasn't easy but *we* wanted what was best for you.

SYLVIA. You robbed me of the chance to say goodbye.

JULIE. You can't tell me you'd rather have stayed round here.

Been a no one. Crumbled house round the corner, two fat kids and a husband who...

He never wanted *more*. He'd have dragged you home and kept you there for him.

I'm not selfish, you know. I'm not.

I tried. Tried to give him everything he wanted but when we

when we couldn't, when we thought we couldn't, I started my own life. I *finally* started something.

Then out of nowhere, there you came.

And I could have been so angry.

But I gave it to you instead.

I gave you everything I ever dreamed of, and I am so proud of what you've done with it, I am. You must see that, you must.

Silence.

SYLVIA. Remember. Remember how Dad used to point to the moon and tell me all about how Granddad was living there.

JULIE. It's a good story.

SYLVIA. Auntie Jupiter. All fat and spotty.

Full of gas.

JULIE. Great Uncle Saturn.

SYLVIA. The hula-hooping champion of the world!

Cousin Martia.

JULIE (*laughing*). Yes. He was daft.

SYLVIA. We had a whole family of planets.

JULIE. I always wanted to travel.

SYLVIA. He always wanted to go there.

JULIE. We did a bit.

SYLVIA. His mother too.

JULIE. When the world still wanted us. He loved sangria.

SYLVIA. You should always visit family.

JULIE. Was never fussed myself.

SYLVIA. When you have the chance.

JULIE. You can't hate me for saving you.

Silence.

SYLVIA. I'm going away again.

JULIE. That's good.

SYLVIA. I can't tell you what it is.

JULIE. I understand.

SYLVIA. You'll see it on your precious screen.

Pause.

JULIE. I was here for him, you know. For both of us.

SYLVIA. I miss him.

JULIE. I know. I miss him too. I thought I'd be relieved by now, with all that care, all that effort over with but

Without him's worse.

I won't be far behind.

Pause.

I'm scared, Sylvie.

Promise you'll be here for me. When I go. Promise you'll be here to hold my hand.

Silence.

SYLVIA. What will you do with his ashes?

***

1969

The Party

Dawn.

SYLVIA (*to* THE ASTRONAUT). I don't remember it. Isn't that strange?

I didn't want to tell you beforehand. I didn't want you to stop. And during I was busy. Fixated really. So that really only left the afterwards, the now really. And I don't want it so I can tell everyone. I just want it for me. Cos I don't remember it.

Your name.

It's all just so new, isn't it. We live in a whole new world, now don't we. Possibilities. So much to achieve and to remember, I just can't keep it all in my head and things, some things, get lost. Get pushed out for trying to make more room and I

I want to keep it all in but just haven't got the space.

We're all about space now, aren't we. Exploring. But it gets filled up, doesn't it. I want to have done everything, felt everything, tasted *everything*, the smell the

learning of it all.

But it means forgetting things sometimes, doesn't it. Important things, for like, a second or two. Maybe more.

We should do something. You and me. Find somewhere we've never been to and just do it. Conquer it, for the first time. Claim it as ours. Our space forever.

My first time. It's all about being remembered, isn't it. First times. You mark your name in history, don't you. I used to get up early, in the winter just to be the first to walk in the snow, leave my footprint. Stop me if I'm gabbling, will you, it's just

I feel like something's starting now. Do you? Do you feel like something's started?

***

2017

Sylvia's Hospice

Midnight.

THE ASTRONAUT *stands waiting.*

Silence.

SYLVIA. I still don't remember your name.

Silence.

So you've finally come back for me?

I'd planned what I was going to say here, but I'm tired now.

Will you take me away?

THE ASTRONAUT *holds out his hand.*

SYLVIA *opens her arms wide and begins to float upwards.*

Blackout.

***

Lights fade up to reveal…

1985

A Lecture Theatre, Washington State University, USA

WILLIAM SAFIRE (*reading from a piece of paper*). Fate has ordained that the men who went to the moon to explore in peace will stay on the moon to rest in peace.

They will be mourned by their family and friends. They will be mourned by a Mother Earth.

Every human being will know... there is some corner of another world that is forever mankind.

He lowers the pages and takes his glasses off.

Lights fade and the scene merges until...

***

2056

The Surface of Mars

Radio chatter.

SYLVIA *is standing.*

She stretches out her arm and opens her hand.

Ash scatters across the ground.

A Nick Hern Book

In Event of Moone Disaster first published as a paperback original in Great Britain in 2017 by Nick Hern Books Limited, The Glasshouse, 49a Goldhawk Road, London W12 8QP, in association with Theatre503

In Event of Moone Disaster copyright © 2017 Andrew Thompson

Andrew Thompson has asserted his right to be identified as the author of this work

Cover photograph by David Schermann

Designed and typeset by Nick Hern Books, London
Printed in Great Britain by Mimeo Ltd, Huntingdon, Cambridgeshire PE29 6XX

A CIP catalogue record for this book is available from the British Library

ISBN 978 1 84842 700 6

CAUTION All rights whatsoever in this play are strictly reserved. Requests to reproduce the text in whole or in part should be addressed to the publisher.

Amateur Performing Rights Applications for performance, including readings and excerpts, by amateurs in the English language throughout the world should be addressed to the Performing Rights Manager, Nick Hern Books, The Glasshouse, 49a Goldhawk Road, London W12 8QP, *tel* +44 (0)20 8749 4953, *email* rights@nickhernbooks.co.uk, except as follows:

Australia: Dominie Drama, 8 Cross Street, Brookvale 2100, *tel* (2) 9938 8686, *fax* (2) 9938 8695, *email* drama@dominie.com.au

New Zealand: Play Bureau, PO Box 9013, St Clair, Dunedin 9047, *tel* (3) 455 9959, *email* info@playbureau.com

South Africa: DALRO (pty) Ltd, PO Box 31627, 2017 Braamfontein, *tel* (11) 712 8000, *fax* (11) 403 9094, *email* theatricals@dalro.co.za

USA and Canada: Casarotto Ramsay and Associates Ltd, see details below

Professional Performing Rights Applications for performance by professionals in any medium and in any language throughout the world (including by stock companies in the USA and Canada) should be addressed to Casarotto Ramsay and Associates Ltd, Waverley House, 7–12 Noel Street, London W1F 8GQ, *fax* +44 (0)20 7287 9128, *email* agents@casarotto.co.uk

No performance of any kind may be given unless a licence has been obtained. Applications should be made before rehearsals begin. Publication of this play does not necessarily indicate its availability for amateur performance.

Woodland
CARBON
www.woodlandcarbon.co.uk
NICK HERN BOOKS
Printed on Carbon-Captured paper

www.nickhernbooks.co.uk

facebook.com/nickhernbooks

twitter.com/nickhernbooks